An Invitation from BRF

In 2001 it will be ten ye████████████████████████ck in
January 1997, a Service████████████████████████n in
Westminster Abbey, Lor████████████████████y. In
2001 there will be four s████████████████████ving,
and we are delighted that████████████████████ our
preachers:

Saturday 12 May 2001

St Helen's Parish Church, St Helen's, Merseyside at 2.00pm
Preacher: The Rt Revd Dr James Jones, Bishop of Liverpool

Saturday 9 June 2001

Christchurch, Clifton, Bristol at 2.00pm
Preacher: The Revd Baroness Richardson of Calow OBE

Saturday 22 September 2001

Durham Cathedral at 2.00pm
Preacher: The Rt Revd Michael Turnbull, Bishop of Durham

Saturday 27 October 2001

Bury St Edmunds Cathedral at 2.00pm
*Preacher: The Revd Canon Dr Christina Baxter, Principal,
St John's Nottingham*

These services will provide an opportunity for all of us involved
with BRF in whatever way—readers, subscribers, supporters,
authors, contributors to the Bible reading notes, trustees and staff
—to celebrate and give thanks for all that has taken place within
BRF over the past decade.

We hope very much that many of you, the readers of our Bible
reading notes, will be able to join us on one (or more) of these important occasions, and we extend a very warm invitation to you all.

Admission to the services will be by ticket, and you are welcome to
apply for as many tickets as you would like. If you wish to bring
friends or are able to bring a group from your church, we would be
delighted.

Please complete the form overleaf to apply for tickets.

(PLEASE PRINT)

Name: _____

Address: _____

_____

_____ Postcode: _____

Telephone (day): _____

Telephone (evening): _____

E-mail: _____

Please send me tickets for the following service(s):

Qty

☐ Saturday 12 May 2001, St Helen's Parish Church, 2.00pm _____

☐ Saturday 9 June 2001, Christchurch, Clifton, Bristol, 2.00pm _____

☐ Saturday 22 Sept 2001, Durham Cathedral, 2.00pm _____

☐ Saturday 27 Oct 2001, Bury St Edmunds Cathedral, 2.00pm _____

Total number of tickets: _____

Please send your completed form to:

2001 Service Ticket Dept
BRF
Peter's Way
Sandy Lane West
Oxford
OX4 6HG

Ticket applications will be processed strictly on a first-come, first-served basis. We will advise you if your application arrives after all the tickets have been allocated. If you do not hear from us, you may assume that tickets have been reserved for you as requested, and these will be despatched approximately three weeks before each service takes place.

Day by Day with God

Bible Readings for Women

JANUARY–APRIL 2001

Christina Press
Bible Reading Fellowship
Tunbridge Wells/Oxford

Copyright © 2001 Christina Press and BRF

BRF, Peter's Way, Sandy Lane West, Oxford, OX4 5HG

First published in Great Britain 2001

ISBN 1 84101 131 2

Jacket design: JAC Design for Print, Crowborough

Trade representation in UK:
Lion Publishing plc, Peter's Way, Sandy Lane West,
Oxford OX4 5HG

Distributed in Australia by:
Willow Connection, PO Box 288, Brookvale, NSW 2100.
Tel: 02 9948 3957; Fax: 02 9948 8153;
E-mail: info@willowconnection.com.au

Distributed in New Zealand by:
Scripture Union Wholesale, PO Box 760, Wellington
Tel: 04 385 0421; Fax: 04 384 3990; E-mail: suwholesale@clear.net.nz

Distributed in South Africa by:
Struik Book Distributors, PO Box 193, Maitland 7405
Tel: 021 551 5900; Fax: 021 551 1124; E-mail: enquiries@struik.co.za

Acknowledgments

Printed in Great Britain
by Omnia Books Limited, Glasgow

Contents

The Editor writes...

Today is dull and overcast and I am glad to be indoors, working away at my desk. Yet I know that if I take the time to stand and look out of the window, I will see a garden full of colour, even at this time of the year. Bright clumps of early daffodils blowing around in the cold north wind, and a tree covered in delicate pink blossom that seems to defy the coldest weather. But, like the sky, I have been feeling somewhat grey. I have been rushing through the last few weeks, feeling far too busy, harrassed and a bit sorry for myself—definitely not quite the right preparation to sit down and write this Editor's letter for *Day by Day with God* at the beginning of a new year!

Words I needed to hear
Yet when I did sit down to check through the various contributors' notes now ready to be sent on to the copy-editor, words and phrases jumped out of the page at me—words that I needed to read and take note of. And just as the brightness of the daffodils has made the the skies less grey, the notes I have just read have cheered me immensely! I hope this is the effect they will have on you in the busyness or otherwise of your days through the first four months of 2001.

One of our new writers, Elizabeth Rundle, has contributed helpful readings on trust. She has a card pinned up in her kitchen which says, 'Look back with gratitude, look forward with hope and look upward with confidence' (see note for 27 January). I like that! Just right for the beginning of another year.

Another new contributor, Cynthia Tay, when writing on 'joy', also talks about words on a wall—this time a plaque on the wall of a friend's house which says, 'Joy is not the absence of sorrows. It's the presence of the Lord' (see note for 6 April). Do you have a special text or saying that you have found helpful pinned up somewhere in your home? Why not write in and share it with us—perhaps saying why you find the words helpful.

Thank you for writing

Thank you, again, to all those who have written in with comments about the notes—it is so encouraging, and *helpful*. We want to provide a resource for women of all ages and in so many different situations and circumstances. Your ideas, advice and input are noted and valued—so keep writing!

Mary Reid

Contributors

Diana Archer has three young children and a degree in religious studies, and has served in Japan as a missionary. She has worked in the publishing world as a freelance editor and writer. Her book *Who'd Plant a Church?* has been highly acclaimed.

Anne Coomes has been a journalist for the Church of England for nearly twenty years, does freelance communications work for various dioceses and has written five books. Together with the well-known artist Taffy Davies, she has launched www.parishpump.co.uk, a website providing a wide variety of articles for parish magazine editors. She holds a degree in theology, and is Reader for her parish in north Cheshire.

Rosemary Green has an international speaking ministry, sometimes alongside her husband Michael. Her highly praised book *God's Catalyst* distils her wisdom and experience gained through many years of prayer counselling. She is on the pastoral staff of Wycliffe Theological College in Oxford.

Margaret Killingray is a tutor at the London Institute for Contemporary Christianity. She has assisted Dr John Stott and others in running Christian Impact conferences here and overseas. Margaret and her husband, David, have three daughters and five grandchildren.

Jennifer Rees Larcombe, one of Britain's best-loved Christian authors and speakers, lives in Kent. She contributes regularly to Christian magazines, including a problem page, and has recently published a book on the ministry of angels, a children's Bible story book and an account of her dramatic recovery, *Unexpected Healing*. See page 146 for an extract from her latest book for BRF, *Beauty from Ashes*.

Christine Leonard lives in Surrey with her husband and two teenage children. She writes books for both adults and children; most tell the true stories of ordinary Christians who have done extraordinary things. She is the Vice President of the Association of Christian Writers.

Elaine Pountney is a dynamic conference and retreat speaker, presently working as a management consultant in the corporate world. She is married to Michael, an Anglican priest, and has two married daughters, one in England and one on Vancouver Island. Elaine enjoys playing tennis and knitting Aran sweaters for her grandchild.

Mary Reid is the editor of *Day by Day with God*. She is a trained teacher and a former magazine and book editor. She is married to Bishop Gavin Reid; they have two sons, a daughter and four grandchildren.

Elizabeth Rundle is a Methodist minister. Most of her life was spent in Cornwall, and she and her husband were married for twenty-one years before he died in 1988. She has written five books of daily readings and led pilgrimages to the Holy Land. She has contributed to religious programmes on radio and television, including 'Prayer for the Day' on Radio 4.

Cynthia Tay, a teacher by profession, has had varied experiences growing up in Malaysia, studying in Canada and living and working in Singapore. She is a teacher of the Word, a counsellor and a conference speaker, sometimes alongside her husband, Moses, the retired Bishop of Singapore. They have two children in the medical and dental professions, and three grandchildren.

Sandra Wheatley lives in County Durham, is a qualified nurse and was diagnosed with multiple sclerosis thirteen years ago. She is single, lives alone, but is not lonely as family and friends live nearby. She has a variety of interests which keep her actively involved in the lives of those around her.

Contributors are identified by their initials at the bottom of each page.

A Morning Prayer

Thank you, heavenly Father,
for this new day.
Be with me now
in all I do
and think
and say,
that it will be to your glory.

Amen

Headline news

The beginning of the gospel about Jesus Christ, the Son of God.

Headlines are meant to grab our attention. They are written in huge print—they convey a lot of meaning in a few words. Those nameless people who work in newspaper offices spend their days using words so concisely and cleverly that they will make thousands of us want to buy the paper to read the news that follows the headline.

This is exactly what Mark is doing in this first sentence of his Gospel. He intends to make his readers sit up and take notice. The significance of the words he uses would not have been lost on the people he was writing for. 'The beginning...' had a ring of authority—this was something new and important. And they would certainly have understood the use of the word 'gospel', which was used to announce an event so significant that it would make a change in world history. Jesus is the Christ—the Messiah—the promised deliverer of God's people. And then the breathtaking conclusion to his headline—'Son of God'. This Jesus was no ordinary man.

Mark was almost certainly the first to write a book about Jesus. He grew up in Jerusalem (Acts 12:12), went with Saul (Paul) and Barnabas on a mission (Acts 12:25), and also spent time with Peter, when he was in prison (1 Peter 5:13). While he was with Peter he would have heard vivid, first-hand accounts of the life and work of Jesus. And nearly two thousand years later you and I have the benefit of reading Mark's account of the good news of Jesus.

Today we begin in earnest the second millennium since the birth of Christ. The headlines in our newspapers, most days, show us that we live in a world that seems unaware and uninterested in Jesus. Perhaps the most important New Year resolution we can make as we begin 2001 is to ensure the good news of Jesus is known by those around us.

Dear Father, help me to make Jesus 'headline news' in my life this year.

MR

A signpost

John wore clothing made of camel's hair, with a leather belt round his waist, and he ate locusts and wild honey.

My first reaction to an invitation is not 'How nice!' but 'What should I wear?' This always irritates me because it isn't that I want to make sure I will stand out as 'the best dressed woman'—just the opposite, in fact. I want to merge quietly into the crowd.

Some years ago my husband and I went to a reception to welcome Dr Billy Graham to Sheffield. One of my sons decided to come too, and he cycled about fifty miles to Sheffield from his university, arriving on time but hot and sweaty, wearing a T-shirt, shorts and cycling shoes. And he stood out in that crowded room!

Now my son didn't deliberately wear different clothes so that he would be noticed. But in our passage today, John did. His clothing was modelled on the prophet Elijah (2 Kings 1:8). He had an important message to deliver, so he certainly wanted to be noticed. People flocked to see this amazing sight. We read in verse 5 that 'all the people of Jerusalem went out to him'! He preached an uncompromising message: they had to repent (turn away) from their sins and be baptized. But John knew that it was not through him that they could be restored as God's people; he pointed them to someone 'more powerful' still to come. John's role was to herald the one who would baptize them with the Holy Spirit.

John acted as a signpost pointing to Jesus. Perhaps we need to do the same. I don't think we need to wear weird clothes and eat locusts and honey. We just need to be brave enough to let our friends see that we follow Jesus.

Always be prepared to give an answer to everyone who asks you to give the reason for the hope that you have (1 Peter 3:15).

MR

Recognition

At that time Jesus came from Nazareth in Galilee and was baptized by John in the Jordan.

Would you recognize Jesus if you were to meet him walking along the street, or going round the supermarket?

I have just been to an amazing art exhibition in London on the image of Christ. Artists through the centuries have painted what they thought Jesus looked like. One gallery concentrated on portraits 'not made with hands': a small representation of the Turin Shroud, and the 'Veronica'—a piece of cloth which is believed to bear an impression of Christ ever since it was used to wipe his face when he was carrying his cross. Some artists made Jesus seem sad, others attempted to emphasize his power and divine status. As I looked at all these different images of the face of Christ I wondered how much other people's ideas had affected my expectations, and whether I would recognize him if I met him in an unexpected place.

John was expecting this special someone to make himself known soon. He was expecting someone more powerful than himself, someone who would make him feel totally unworthy (v. 7). Yet when Jesus arrived he looked just like any other Galilean, just one among the crowd lining the bank of the muddy Jordan, come to be baptized by John. It was not until Jesus had been baptized, and was coming up out of the water, that all this ordinariness changed. The heavens were 'torn open and the Spirit descended on him'. A voice from heaven said, 'You are my Son, whom I love; with you I am well pleased.'

Jesus was no ordinary Galilean. He was God's Son. In Mark's account of this event, God speaks directly to Jesus, and the Holy Spirit descended on him 'like a dove'—as a dove would descend, gently.

Jesus' public ministry had begun. He would no longer go unrecognized in the crowd.

Read Matthew 25:31–40.

MR

13

Follow me...

'Come, follow me,' Jesus said... At once they left their nets and followed him.

Simon and Andrew had almost certainly met Jesus before (see John 1:35–42). They were fishermen by trade, as were James and John, the sons of Zebedee. They all had a family business to run. They had responsibilities. Yet when Jesus said, 'Follow me', they didn't hesitate. They left all the familiar security behind to follow this Jesus, who had said he would make them 'fishers of men'—whatever that meant!

There are always two sides to a decision to follow Jesus. The disciples had to be prepared to leave home, and jobs they knew how to do, for a future that was unfamiliar and insecure. This seems hard on Zebedee, left to carry on his business with the help of hired hands instead of his sons. And didn't Simon have a wife?

Much later, when Jesus was teaching his disciples about commitment, he said, 'Anyone who loves his father or mother more than me is not worthy of me...' (Matthew 10:37). This verse helps me to get these five verses in Mark into the right perspective. These new disciples weren't neglecting their responsibilities, but they were making it quite clear they were followers of Jesus. They didn't have to be scholars, or theologians, or even amazingly clever. Their qualification for discipleship was that they put Jesus first in their lives—and they trusted Jesus with their future.

Ever since those first disciples obeyed Jesus' invitation to follow him, millions have followed their example. The invitation that Jesus gave then he still gives today, and there comes a point in the life of every Christian when a decision has to be made. It doesn't have to involve physically leaving home and family, but it does have to involve deciding to put Jesus first.

Read Mark 10:28–30.

MR

Authority

The people were amazed at his teaching, because he taught as one who had authority…

I'm not a very good listener. I find it very hard to concentrate on anyone giving a talk, no matter how interesting. Usually I have to make notes to keep my mind focused. But every now and then I hear someone speaking who really makes me sit up and listen.

Jesus had this authority, this special something, that electrified those who were in the synagogue that day in Capernaum. Who was this young man from that insignificant village of Nazareth who could address them so confidently and directly? Normally, whoever was teaching began by saying something like, 'There is a teaching that says…', but this man was talking to them as if the message came from him.

They were already sitting up and taking notice of this new teacher when the man with an evil spirit began causing an unwelcome disturbance. 'What do you want with us, Jesus of Nazareth?' he shouted out. 'I know who you are—the Holy One of God!' I have been in a big service in London when demonstrators have burst through the church door, shouting and blowing whistles—obviously intending to break up the service and make everyone take note of them and their cause. It worked: they very much disrupted the service and the reporters present just wrote about them and not about the service itself! However, Jesus was in complete command of this disturbance. He sternly ordered the spirit to leave—and the people were even more amazed at his authority. Even evil spirits obeyed him.

We are not told exactly what Jesus taught about that day, but the people who had been in the synagogue were sure that Jesus was someone very special. Perhaps he was the Messiah they were all waiting for! Jesus didn't need our modern methods of communication—those who had met him and listened to him talked about him to everyone they met. It wasn't long before everyone in Galilee was talking about this Jesus from Nazareth.

What will you be talking about today?

MR

Finding space

Jesus went off to a solitary place, where he prayed. Simon and his companions went to look for him… 'Everyone is looking for you!'

I think everyone reading this today will be able to relate to this situation. Jesus has slipped away from the house very early in the morning to find a bit of peace and quiet to pray. Simon and company, instead of realizing that Jesus needed to be on his own, had managed to track him down and reminded Jesus that everyone was looking for him.

Who hasn't sneaked off, when life has got too busy, to find a little bit of space in the day? We all need time for ourselves—and, even more important, we all need time to pray. Once, when I found life had got too overwhelming, I left the car unlicensed in the garage and got out my bike to cycle to school each day. It gave me half-an-hour to myself between the demands of home and school each morning, and another half-an-hour on the way home in the afternoon. I must have been an interesting sight—a middle-aged lady pedalling along on an over-laden bike, muttering away to herself. Any observers weren't to know that I was praying!

The disciples had come to remind Jesus that he was needed back in Capernaum. But Jesus had other plans. He needed to move on—there were others who needed to hear his message.

I wonder how the disciples felt. It must have been exciting to see Jesus healing people and driving out demons (vv. 32–34). Everything was happening. Jesus was a success. They had been right to follow him! Did they really want to stay among all the 'buzz', or were they ready to move on? We are not told. But Jesus knew he had to move on.

Two things from this passage:
1) Make space to pray today.
2) Be positive if you are in the middle of change (job, house, etc)—it's a new challenge.

MR

A prophet and a problem

How long, O Lord, must I call for help, but you do not listen? Or cry out to you, 'Violence!' but you do not save? Why do you make me look at injustice? Why do you tolerate wrong?

I confess to a penchant for highlighting the nice bits in the biblical prophets' books, and skating over the fire and thunder. When I need strength for the day I am drawn to words that inspire and comfort. And yes, I had approached Habakkuk thus and thereby missed the whole point. I repent.

For on closer reading, I discovered a man, living about 600BC, who is after my own heart. Look at the way he begins his chat with God. No messing about. He goes straight to the point of what is bothering him. And the subjects he raises are ones which I wrestle with too.

Habakkuk is writing against a background of Judah, his country loved by God but unfaithful to God. Habakkuk's anguish is caused by his fellow countrymen's rejection of their unique covenant with God. God has promised them so much, if they will just worship him and keep their side of the agreement. But all around him, Habakkuk sees a society in decay, a people who have turned from God and good and run after evil. So Habakkuk voices his complaint. How can you tolerate this, God? How can you let it go on? The violence is escalating; the injustice hurts me to see. Why don't you do something?

Why doesn't God stop the suffering? For those who find it hard to believe that God is really there and really good, this is a major stumbling-block. Isn't it also the cry of our own hearts when we see the pain in our world? I could not have phrased it better myself, Habakkuk. Exactly.

These are deeply penetrating questions, yet Habakkuk does not hesitate to address them directly to God. What do you do with yours?

Read Psalm 73.

DA

God replies

Look at the nations and watch—and be utterly amazed. For I am going to do something in your days that you would not believe, even if you were told. I am raising up the Babylonians, that ruthless and impetuous people, who sweep across the whole earth to seize dwelling-places not their own.

These verses may not strike you as particularly edifying ones for a morning quiet time. I think they were not what Habakkuk wanted to hear over his bowl of cornflakes, either. The risk of truly engaging with God and listening to him is that we may not like what he has to say. God's reply to Habakkuk's agonized questioning was to assure him of coming judgment. The wickedness Habakkuk so despaired of in his precious nation would not go for ever unchecked. Indeed, the destruction of Jerusalem in 597BC prophesied here would be a cataclysmic event for the Judeans, triggering a national and religious crisis.

Judgment. Who wants it? When we also cry out for justice, do we realize what we are calling down on ourselves? For none of us is innocent. Who wants to pay for their misdeeds? Wouldn't we rather get away with it, and no one ever know? I have a wonderful spoof diet sheet magneted to my freezer, just to keep things in perspective. One of its 'rules' reassures that food eaten in secret has no calories. If no one sees you, it is OK. Anything goes.

But if nothing matters, if there is no reckoning, ever, then we really are in trouble. If any behaviour is acceptable, then any evil is also. The world runs wild. It seems that while we hate judgment, we actually need it. The concept of a day of judgment is currently unpopular in the West, but the consequences of writing it off seem dire indeed. We need to know that one day, all of our wickedness will earn God's decree: 'Enough!'

Dear Father, help me to be absolutely honest with you. Amen.
Read Ephesians 6:7–8 for some positive motivation.

DA

A prophet confused

O Lord, you have appointed them to execute judgment; O Rock, you have ordained them to punish. Your eyes are too pure to look on evil; you cannot tolerate wrong. Why then do you tolerate the treacherous? Why are you silent while the wicked swallow up those more righteous than themselves?

Have you ever prayed earnestly about a situation and it immediately got worse? I wonder if this was what Habakkuk faced. He was initially heartbroken at the triumph of wickedness in his society, but God's reply to his accusation brings more complications. Wait a minute, God—you are going to do something about the wrongdoers by what? By raising up a notoriously evil nation to pulverize Judah? This doesn't make sense! How can two wrongs make a right? How can you be holy and yet instigate this destruction?

Habakkuk is wrestling with fundamental questions as to the very nature of God. Unique among the prophets, his discourse is always *to* God *about* his country. He does not address prophecy to Judah. His tussle is on their behalf, but is with God alone. He is a brave man. These searching questions do not necessarily come readily to us, especially if we are insecure in our relationship with God. We shy away from rocking the boat for our own sake. But Habakkuk was not afraid. He was not put off by God's baffling reply, even though it intensified his pain and confusion. He did not make excuses for God or water down the problem. He said it as he saw it.

So returning to those frustrating prayers that seem to backfire, be encouraged by Habakkuk. We are not the first to have these reactions to God. Take your complaint straight to your heavenly Father. Be honest. Be angry. But be with him and give him a chance to reply.

Dear Father, so much about life does not make sense to us—so much about the way you work. But please let these things draw us closer to you, in questioning, and not keep us away. Amen.
Read Job 7:17–21.

DA

A prophet answered

For the revelation awaits an appointed time; it speaks of the end and will not prove false. Though it linger, wait for it; it will certainly come and will not delay... The cup from the Lord's right hand is coming round to you, and disgrace will cover your glory.

Isn't it lovely that God answers Habakkuk? Bear in mind that Habakkuk has implicitly accused God of inconsistency to his character, and of impurity. Yet there is no sense of an impatient, 'Be quiet Habakkuk, you do not know what you are talking about.' Instead, God graciously spells out that he is noting every one of the Babylonians' transgressions (2:4–20) and that they will be punished for them (see above). The executioners will themselves stand trial. They too will be condemned, not just for their cruelty, but also for their idolatry.

This must have made Habakkuk feel a bit better. It would be blatantly unfair if the Babylonians were to destroy Judah and not be held to account. Habakkuk was still left with questions, but no longer could he edge towards accusing God of not noticing and not caring. The time would come when God would respond. Habakkuk still had to trust, however, that it would happen as God said.

Waiting for God to act has to be one of the hardest things he ever asks us to do. Waiting on God, until the time is right, is so difficult. Our instant consumer society is often blamed—we want it now!—but impatience has to be deeply rooted in the human psyche. Habakkuk had to wait about sixty-six years until Babylon fell, and we do not know if he ever saw it. But it did happen. Meanwhile, he had to struggle on in the same situation, with only the promise that change was ahead. Not easy. Not even sure that the promised retribution was the solution he wanted. But at least he and God were talking.

Those who wait for the Lord shall renew their strength (Isaiah 40:31, NRSV).
Read Habakkuk 1 and 2 for the overall picture.

DA

Serious sin

Woe to him who says to wood, 'Come to life!' Or to lifeless stone, 'Wake up!' Can it give guidance? It is covered with gold and silver; there is no breath in it. But the Lord is in his holy temple; let all the earth be silent before him.

Habakkuk had worked out that the Babylonians' trust in themselves was offensive to God (2:16), but I wonder if he had picked up the strength of God's revulsion. All of the prophets wax eloquent about the sin of idolatry, so Habakkuk is not unusual in this. However, dip into the pages of any of the Old Testament prophets, and you will find idolatry condemned not just in foreigners but more poignantly among the Israelites too (for example, Hosea). Indeed the history of Israel seesaws between the nation's trust in and love of God; and then their abandonment of him and worship of idols.

Here in Habakkuk, the sin of idolatry is up there with violence and depravity. Because the latter are so easy to see, do they matter more to us than the underlying desertion of God? Habakkuk wrings his hands first over the violation of human rights and only later acknowledges the desecration of divine worship that has been perpetrated. Yet this latter tears God's heart apart.

It is easy to denounce biblical characters for venerating carved chunks of wood. But do we not have equivalents? It is so simple to worship something there in front of you. It is said that the way we spend our time and money exposes what we worship. Now there is an uncomfortable challenge. Where do we waste the loyalty and energy that properly belong to our heavenly Father alone? Why do we miss out on the glorious freedom of placing all our trust in the one who cares for us like no other?

This sin of idolatry seems to be constructed like an onion—layers and layers to unpeel and repent of. It is horrendous how deceptive we can be, even to ourselves. Thank God for grace!

Treat yourself to Romans 8.

DA

Faith is everything

See, he is puffed up; his desires are not upright—but the righteous will live by his faith.

I think God goes to great lengths to reassure Habakkuk that he is fully aware of his situation. I find it so easy to fall into the trap of thinking that God is at best preoccupied or at worst just does not care any more. But because Habakkuk took the time and courage to be honest with God, it gave God the chance to respond. Although Habakkuk still had to wait, he now knew that God had a plan.

In today's verse, God deliberately contrasts the Babylonians' self-satisfaction with the life of faith in him. Despite their current earthly power, the Babylonians would ultimately be condemned. But those who waited on and trusted in God would ultimately live. There must have been others like Habakkuk in Judah, watching and wondering as their nation fell apart around their ears. They needed the encouragement to hang on in there for God. Their faith foreshadows our New Testament invitation that salvation comes by faith alone.

I reckon it is impossible to live the Christian life without facing times like those Habakkuk faced—times when life disintegrates and God seems a million miles away. The exhortation to keep going recurs frequently throughout the Bible. God knows the going gets tough. Take heart from his patient treatment of Habakkuk. The very fact that Habakkuk took his agonies to God, rather than turning away, demonstrates his underlying faith. Sometimes that is all we can offer. But it is enough. Habakkuk's faith was thoroughly vindicated. So will ours be.

If it is what you need, take time today to pray for encouragement. Be open to receive it.

DA

The big picture

For the earth will be filled with the knowledge of the glory of the Lord, as the waters cover the sea… But the Lord is in his holy temple; let all the earth be silent before him.

I suspect that God breathes a sigh of relief when we finally drag ourselves into his presence, exhausted with our life's burdens. Perhaps you are better at running straight to the source of true help than I am, but I have found that once I am there, it is as if God says, 'OK, I hear you. I love you. Now that I have your attention, there are things I want to mention…'

Habakkuk began with a complaint that God was not doing anything about local evil. God expands his vision beyond Judah and shows him a vision of the whole world responding to his glory:

'See the big picture, Habakkuk. One day the ends of the earth will know I am who I say I am. You questioned my purity. Realize that before my holiness all will be silenced. Let me lift the curtain and give you a glimpse of my majesty. There is so much more than you ever dreamed of.'

Our vision is naturally blinkered and prejudiced. Like Habakkuk, we are only human. We see things from the limited position of being one person in one time with one life. We need God to restore our perspective again and again. We need him to reveal things from his angle rather than ours, like the difference between viewing a skyscraper from the ground or from an aeroplane. We need to respond to our heavenly Father in love and trust and gaze into his eyes for a while. Then when we look back down at our circumstances, we stand a chance of seeing God in them.

Even though at times life gets me down,
Pain breaks through my living and threatens to destroy me deep inside,
Still, my Saviour, you protect me.
You take me by the hand and lead me through the valley
To the place where there is joy.

G. Archer and A. Rayner

DA

More, Lord!

Lord, I have heard of your fame; I stand in awe of your deeds, O Lord. Renew them in our day, in our time make them known; in wrath remember mercy.

The more I dig into Habakkuk's book, the more I like it. Here is Habakkuk's prayerful response to all God has shown him. He has moved from anguish and despair to worship. These words feel very different to his initial litany of 'Why?'s. I suspect, if pressed, Habakkuk would not have been able to produce watertight answers to his original agonized questions, but his viewpoint has changed. Now those questions are subordinate to what he has learned of God, and to his worship of and trust in him.

Is this how it often has to be? We come to God with questions, wanting instant answers and relief from our pain. But God draws us closer to himself and quietly changes the agenda. Like Habakkuk, we are invited to see the bigger picture and trust again.

Habakkuk's opening cry here meets an 'Oh yes!' inside me when I read the words. It is that little word 'renew'. It is the voice of longing—longing for more of God to be seen and experienced by more people, more of the time. It is the parallel recognition that yes, we deserve wrath because of our sin, as Judah did; but yes, we know the mercy of God is like nothing else we experience. This little prayer expresses beautifully a totally adequate prayer for the whole world for all time. That God would renew his acts of mercy in every generation and in every life—isn't that what we long for?

How does God answer this longing?

You have chosen me, set my life apart
To declare the wonder of your name.
Awesome mighty God, Saviour, Friend and Lord,
Of your love and grace I will proclaim.
Andrew and Wendy Rayner

DA

24

'But-if-not' faith

*Though the fig-tree does not bud and there are no grapes on
the vines, though the olive crop fails and the fields produce no
food, though there are no sheep in the pen and no cattle in the
stalls, yet I will rejoice in the Lord, I will be joyful in God my
Saviour.*

Habakkuk has made a tremendous spiritual journey in the course
of his writing. His faith in God has expanded exponentially, until
now he can declare it intact in the face of any calamity.

This, to me, is our greatest challenge. To walk in faith in the
pitch black, if you like. To keep believing when all the evidence
screams in denial of God's care or activity. These verses are
especially poignant for me. Put to music, they comprised the
favourite song of a friend of ours. This friend was killed recently
in a car crash. He was generous to a fault, and spent his life
working on behalf of others. Why, Lord? Yet his special song
encourages us to keep on believing, even without answers.

This is real-life, gut-level faith. It is not a crutch. It is not easy.
It is 'But-if-not' faith, as Shadrach declared when poised above
the fiery furnace in Daniel 3:17–18: 'The God we serve is able to
save us from it, and he will rescue us from your hand, O king.
But even if he does not, we want you to know, O king, that we
will not serve your gods or worship the image of gold you have
set up.'

'But-if-not' faith hangs on anyway, even if there is no fruit for
our labours, or joy for our lives. It trusts God at the deepest level,
regardless of the consequences.

Is this kind of faith only possible when we have, like
Habakkuk, tasted the ultimate goodness of God? I may be selling us short here. Perhaps it is just a decision. But total abandonment to God can be hard. Is the answer to invite God to
come so close that trust is inevitable?

Take time to respond.

DA

A prophet at peace

The Sovereign Lord is my strength; he makes my feet like the feet of a deer, he enables me to go on the heights.

So Habakkuk ends his prose on a high point. Having started in the depths, he finishes with an unequivocal declaration of confidence in God. The Almighty God will be his personal resource for living. No matter how difficult the terrain, God will give him all he needs for balance, poise and progress. He can confidently head for the best mountain views. He can enjoy unsurpassable exhilaration. He can go for gold.

I have a little theory here. I wonder if we can only join in with Habakkuk's joyful assertion if we have passed through verses 17 and 18 first. How can God be our strength unless we have truly thrown ourselves on him? How can we bounce with confidence up to the highest spiritual peaks if we still prevaricate as to whether God really is trustworthy or not? How can we go for the climb with gusto, if we are all the time wondering if the ropes will hold?

But once we have decided that God is to be trusted at every level—for life and death, plenty and want, joy and pain—then we are free to aim for the top. To live life to the full. To know his presence, and experience his strength for it all.

No, of course I have not got it all sorted. I wish I had. But every so often the mist clears and it looks so simple and obvious. When the cloud returns, I grope for a good foothold, and I need friends, prayer and encouragement to hold me steady. Habakkuk has, however, helped. I hope that God has ministered to you through him as well.

Settle yourself with your favourite drink and read through Habakkuk again. Let God highlight the bits he wants to, just for you.

DA

Weeds

Jesus told them another parable: 'The kingdom of heaven is like a man who sowed good seed in his field. But while everyone was sleeping, his enemy came and sowed weeds among the wheat, and went away. When the wheat sprouted and formed ears, then the weeds also appeared.

Oh, the frustration! The house we have moved to has a garden, so I am discovering how green my fingers are. Not very, so far. I have quickly learned that the magic of growth does not work automatically. Care, attention and some basic marrying of soil to appropriate plant seem to be vital. I am on a steep learning curve.

I am also fascinated by how often Jesus uses gardening and agricultural analogies to illustrate the kingdom of God. Now that I am getting dirt under my own fingernails, I appreciate more why he does so. The parallels are impossible to leave alone. It is all there—the growth, the pruning, the fruit—the kingdom of God. The frustration I am experiencing in my wretched attempts at gardening are nothing compared to the frustrations of the growth of the kingdom.

We sow in good faith. We give out, we pray, we yearn for others to know Jesus, we struggle with our witnessing. We care for others in his name, and we donate our money. Then along comes disappointment. The church plant does not thrive. Our neighbour refuses our friendship. A friend rejects a new start with God and her life disintegrates. A project to the glory of God is hijacked by human greed. We wonder where and why it all went wrong.

We cannot always see the whole picture. We are not always aware of all the influences at work. All we do know is that there is not as much harvest as we planted for. It is hard to bear, but take Jesus' parable here as a lesson in reality. This is how it is sometimes, because weeds grow where we least want them. Just look at a garden.

Dear Father, help me to face reality, as Jesus did. Amen.

DA

Enemy action

The owner's servants came to him and said, 'Sir, didn't you sow good seed in your field? Where then did the weeds come from?' 'An enemy did this,' he replied.

My early Christian training was peppered with references to battles and warfare. I was left in no doubt that I had joined an army that was fighting in enemy-occupied territory. It was clear that the earth is the Lord's (Psalm 24:1), but also that the prince of this world was a usurper out to wreak havoc (John 12:31).

At first the concept of throwing in my lot with the winning side in a cosmic struggle was exciting and inspiring. But as time went on, I discovered that Jesus' parable was all too accurate. The weeds are real. The enemy is a force to be reckoned with, even if his time is limited. The wounds hurt. The victims do fall. The battle is not fun.

Well, Jesus did try to tell us. If the Son of God himself warns us about opposition then we would do well to take heed. Jesus does deal in reality, without exception. Never did he consign the devil to fanciful thinking or childish pranks.

Now I do not claim to have all the answers but I do believe it is worth hammering out a solid theology on this one. After all, if a malevolent force is not at work, then whence evil? While there are obvious dangers in assigning every banana skin to the work of the devil, there has to be a balanced approach out there somewhere. Jesus was not fazed by the existence of the devil, and nor should we be. Jesus teaches us that bad will grow alongside good and so we should not be surprised when it does. Perhaps recognizing that reality will protect us from severe disappointment and unrealistic expectations. And in the meantime we can learn how to deal with it.

Dear Father, thank you that you promised your Holy Spirit would lead us into truth. Please guard our hearts and minds as we wrestle with difficult concepts. Amen.
Read John 14:6.

DA

Assault?

The servants asked him, 'Do you want us to go and pull them up?' 'No,' he answered, 'because while you are pulling the weeds, you may root up the wheat with them.'

Now here is where my garden analogy breaks down. I can rush out and pull out weeds to my heart's content any time I like (as long as it is not raining, the ground is soft and I feel in the mood…). But Jesus restrains us from the same approach regarding the kingdom of God. 'Not a good idea,' he says. 'You'll whip out the good with the bad. Leave them both to grow.'

Bit tricky, this. My instinct, if I have actually managed to spot something going wrong, is to rush in and fix it. If I can distinguish quite clearly the bad from the good, I want to uproot it. But God knows my gardening skills are limited. I would wreck the whole plot. Always, always we must wait for God's timing. Like the servants in the parable, we see only the immediate problem. God is looking to the future and the ultimate harvest. Servant-like, we volunteer to sort stuff out for God. But he encourages patience.

There are times to act, to be sure. But if it truly is necessary to challenge something of evil intent, we must be very certain we are obeying the head gardener's instructions or we will find ourselves face down in the mud, having caused even more damage. The best solution is to get to know the head gardener so well that his ways become ours, and we would not dream of plucking a leaf without his approval.

If any of you lacks wisdom, he should ask God, who gives generously to all without finding fault, and it will be given to him (James 1:5).

Dear Father, sometimes I get so worried about things, it is hard to think straight. Help me learn to wait on you and hear your guiding voice in the midst of the tumult. Amen.

DA

Harvest

*Let both grow together until the harvest. At that time I will tell
the harvesters: First collect the weeds and tie them in bundles to
be burned; then gather the wheat and bring it into my barn.*

It is so hard to wait. It is hard enough to wait for good things
coming up, even more so when we see evil running rampant
worldwide, and no answers yet. Has anyone yet been born who
has not railed against the injustice of the world and longed for
change? If God is there, why doesn't he do something?

If we have read our Bible and picked up God's reassurances of
an end point in time when all wrongs will be accounted for, it
makes a difference to how we act now. God's care is such that
not one tear is shed without him noticing (Psalm 126:5) and his
authority is such that his Son can confidently predict a wonderful harvest, untainted by evil. The here and now is not all there
is. In the end justice will prevail. God is sovereign.

But the waiting is hard. It seems we lose too many skirmishes
while we wait for the final victory. We need our captain's commands for our day-to-day deeds. We need to know how to
live while the weeds and wheat are still entangled. Sometimes
they grow so entwined it is hard to tell one from the other.
Sometimes it seems as if the whole field is weeds and the wheat
is stifled. Sometimes we grow despondent and doubt whether
the gardener/captain really knows what he is doing.

Battles and gardens. Enemies and weeds. The adventure of
following Jesus will never be boring. Fortunately my gardening
skills are no reflection of the master gardener's. It will work out.
Just wait and see.

Read Revelation 20—22.

DA

Trust

Commit your way to the Lord; trust in him, and he will act.

The book of Psalms, the great hymn book of Jewish scripture, is a mirror for all our human emotions. These encouraging words from the Psalm 37 are pithy and precise. So easy to say, yet oh, so difficult to enact!

When I am feeling insecure, vulnerable or generally frustrated, it helps me to recall and meditate on those people whose faith I admire. One of those people in my life has been Jan, who, with her husband, responded to God's call to serve with the Mission Aviation Fellowship. This meant giving up a good job, leaving a nice area, training at a Bible college and then leaving family and friends to live for Jesus Christ in a vast African country.

Over the years they have experienced wonderful blessings, adventures and the joy of truly making a difference to people's well-being, both physically and spiritually. There have also been times of disappointment, discouragement and uncertainty for their future. Through all these things, this brief verse from Psalm 37 has sustained Jan, anchoring her faith and motivating her commitment. Here is a family truly committed to the Lord. Their trust has been a powerful witness and the Lord has been seen to act in so many unexpected ways.

Too often I suppose I'm not prepared to trust implicitly—it's as if I feel I need to help the Lord along, to engineer opportunities for his presence to operate. I'm so grateful he has touched my life with people like Jan, for it not only underlines my need for (as the hymn writer put it) 'a childlike, praying trust', but I am inspired by their shining faith.

I am thrilled to hear and see the Lord's work being done, and it spurs me on to look afresh at how my own life has been guided and nurtured.

Dear Lord of all, today, as your trusting and eager child, I commit myself and those I love into your eternal keeping. Amen.

ER

Trust—held fast

Your hand will guide me, your right hand will hold me fast.

Clay is a great medium for self-expression. It's also a good excuse to make a fine mess, all in the name of art. I was once in a group where we were encouraged to portray a recent experience in clay. We then had to look at each other's efforts and guess what they represented. I guessed that the model I looked at was somebody encaged and held against his or her will.

The young man who created the model was, at that time, helping out at a school for children with severe learning and mobility problems. He told us that one afternoon there was great excitement because the school was given a trampoline. Of course, the children could not use the apparatus on their own, so members of staff climbed on with each child to hold them safe. In order that adults and children kept safely to the middle of the trampoline, they painted a large cross in the centre. So, far from representing imprisonment, this model recreated a loving gesture of security and happiness. My judgment had been so wrong.

Many people make wrong judgments about the teaching of Jesus. They suspect the Bible of being a book of restricting rules. In reality, the Bible shows us how ordinary, often anonymous men and women found themselves supported and loved by God like the children in the arms of their carers on the trampoline. They did not need to understand; they just knew they were being supported and kept safe.

Let's pray for situations we have to face where we long to know that Jesus is going to be right there with us, holding us, encouraging us and loving us through them.

Lord, whatever happens, I know I'm safe with you. Amen.

ER

Trust—in God

I do not trust in my bow, my sword does not bring me victory.

Over and over again the inspired writers of scripture make plain the fact that people of God are people of peace. The painful, unlearned lessons of history reveal that trust in weapons of destruction always brings tragedy and tears. We are nevertheless a world dominated by weapons of indescribable evil. Whether we are watching pictures of terrified schoolchildren or the victims of teenage gun madness in America, or seeing victims of landmines, given a high profile by the late Princess Diana, we feel utterly helpless. It seems that the more ingenious we become, the more inhumanely we behave.

The humble psalmist, who only had his bow and sword, recognized their shortcomings. Weapons themselves cannot give us moral victory and weapons will always have unwanted side-effects. But God asks us to depend on him and be part of a world which cares for its inhabitants and shares its vital resources. God does not want us to live in fear, tension and international turmoil.

It's tempting to say that the world was less complicated in biblical days, but the Old Testament graphically records many wars between nations. In all history we can be certain of two things. One, human nature has not changed and, two, nor has God. Our God is the same God in whom millions have put their trust in times of conflict. We, in our time and place, are called to put our faith in Christ before weapons. It's so hard for us to do this because we are conditioned to be self-reliant. This self-reliance steers us away from God, away from the law of love to the worship of ourselves.

Try praying the wise words found in the book of Proverbs: 'Trust in the Lord with all your heart and lean not on your own understanding' (Proverbs 3:5).

ER

Trust—when anxious

'Do not let your hearts be troubled. Trust in God; trust also in me.'

A friend of mine has two sons. They each followed hobbies that they called exhilarating but their mother called downright dangerous! The older son went pot-holing and the younger white-water canoeing. Not being a serious sportsperson of any variety, I cannot begin to see the attraction in these high-adrenaline pursuits. Yet I know that thousands of people find fulfilment in pushing mind and body to the limit. It's their 'fun'.

I'm told abseiling is fun, too. Somehow I can't imagine myself dropping over the edge of some cliff or building for fun, but I've been fascinated to watch other people do it. It's amazing what trust they have in the one who holds the rope at the top. They trust that person with their life.

We all go through experiences which make us feel as though we are going over a cliff of some sort and at these times it is pretty hard to trust the one above us. And yet the Old Testament is peppered with God's promises to be with his people in every situation. Jesus gave words of encouragement to his disciples: they could trust God and they could also trust Jesus, God's Son.

Once 'over the top', the abseilers can no longer see the hands that hold them safely, but they know they have not been abandoned. In one of his hymns, Charles Wesley wrote, 'Give me the childlike, praying trust.' It's only when we learn to trust our Lord in this way that we shall know ourselves held secure in eternal hands. Then we will experience the peace that Jesus promised (John 14:25-27) and be able to enjoy the adventures of life.

Lord, I'm a gold medallist when it comes to anxieties. Help me today, hold me, and teach me how to trust in your strength and power. Amen.

ER

Trust—on life's journey

When Jacob awoke from his sleep, he thought, 'Surely the Lord is in this place, and I was not aware of it.'

Jacob comes across as the Old Testament 'sly guy'. We see his equivalent in many a modern soap, deceitful, thieving and scheming, yet likable with it—a salutary reminder that there is good in the worst of us and bad in the best of us.

Into the middle of the Jacob saga fits the story of the prophetic dream. Jacob wakes up to realize he has had a spiritual encounter with God. As we read of him in a fluster of reverence and guilty conscience, it's amusing to note that Jacob just couldn't resist trying a quick deal with God. If God would look after him then he, Jacob, would worship God and even offer God one tenth of his possessions! It's very tempting to feel superior to Jacob, to look down our noses at his brash audacity; but haven't we all, at some point in our lives, slipped into bargain mode with God ? If he will do such and such, then we will promise to do this and the other thing. The more desperate we are, the more eager we are to make commitments.

Now Jacob was honest enough to admit he'd gone to sleep without giving God a thought. Even so, he woke with a definite awareness of God's presence. This experience was a turning point for Jacob. From that moment he began the journey of spiritual discovery, a journey through baffling difficulties and heartache, from self-sufficiency to dependence and trust in God.

It's a long journey for each of us but Jesus waits to accompany us all the way.

Jesus, I will trust you, trust you with my soul: I'm tired and worn and hopeless, only you can make me whole.

                                                                        ER

Trust—for refuge

I love you, O Lord, my strength… my God is my rock, in whom I take refuge.

Having spent most of my life in the West Country, I feel a great affinity with the rugged landscapes of Dartmoor and Bodmin Moor. The windswept swathes of grass and heather are dominated by the great boulders and identified by the various tors. Some say it is a bleak and forbidding landscape but more people find it a place of strength, of solace even. There is something so reassuring in the grandeur and the knowledge that the hills have been as they are for hundreds of thousands of years. Somehow these wild places trigger our respect for the miracles of nature.

Not only have these same triggers been evident in the ancient authors of the Psalms but the whole idea of strength and stability creeps into our own language and we are proud to speak of relationships as being 'rock-solid'.

A Victorian hymn-writer with a wonderfully Victorian name, Augustus Toplady, was walking in the Mendip Hills when he was caught by quite a violent thunderstorm. As he sheltered in the vast rock-face of Burrington Coomb, he felt that God was protecting him. Afterwards he wrote the hymn 'Rock of Ages, cleft for me, let me hide myself in thee'. There is a beautiful modern hymn which also speaks of God as 'my hiding-place… whenever I am afraid, I will trust in you'.

It is wonderful to know that we are not alone. We can run to our God for 'shelter' and we can 'hide' in his strength. In an ever-changing, complicated and sometimes frightening world, God is our rock.

Read Psalm 121.

ER

Trust—for the future

For I am convinced that neither death nor life, neither angels or demons, neither the present nor the future... nor anything else in all creation will be able to separate us from the love of God that is in Christ Jesus our Lord.

I shall always be grateful to the lady who sent me a beautiful card which said simply, 'Look back with gratitude, look forward with hope and look upward with confidence.' I placed it in the kitchen where I would see it many times a day.

None of us is immune from crises of one kind or another, and when we feel overwhelmed by problems or loss, looking back seems to pile on the recrimination, the regrets and the tears. We can become so bowed down and stressed that we have no energy left to look forward, let alone look upward. Yet move forward we do. Life goes on, and in the end, it takes us along too. In our own time we rejoin the world to find that time has begun the process of healing.

It's then that in looking back we realize we can be thankful and praise God for the miracle of memory. But we musn't just look back, craving for what used to be. We must face the untouched, unfolding future, not with an unrealistic optimism, but with a confidence and trust in God. Paul's letters were messages of hope, just like the little card in my kitchen.

Why not try it for yourself? Take time to look back with gratitude, look to the future with hope and you'll find you are able to look upwards with confidence to your loving creator.

'For I know the plans I have for you,' declares the Lord, 'plans to prosper you and not to harm you, plans to give you hope and a future' (Jeremiah 29:11).

                                                                        ER

The Ten Commandments

And God spoke all these words.

Before starting this new series in which we will look at the Ten Commandments, stop and think for a minute. How many of them can you remember without looking them up? Did you know that Moses brought them down to the people of Israel from a mountain-top meeting with God, only three months after they had left a life of slavery in Egypt? It might be an interesting exercise to ask some of the people you know whether they can recall any of the ten. In a survey a couple of years ago, even ministers found it hard to name them all!

Do read through chapter 20 of Exodus, if you can. As you read and are perhaps reminded again of what the commandments say, what is your reaction to them? Does anything new or surprising strike you about them? God spoke these words to the people of Israel over thirty centuries ago. He wanted them to hear, learn, understand and obey. This is the way he wanted them to live. But what about us?

The laws given to the people of Israel in the Old Testament cannot often be applied as they are, directly to our own lives as Christians in Christian fellowships. We need to look at what other parts of the Bible say in explaining them, especially at the words of Jesus. Do you expect them to challenge you, to make you think again about the way you live? Or are you thinking that there are a lot of other parts of the Bible you would rather read? Getting to grips with the Old Testament laws is a challenge that can be very rewarding, and a good place to start is with these commands.

I want to walk your way every day of my life. These words may be just the ones you want to speak to me each day, Lord. Help me to use my mind and heart to listen.

MK

A solemn covenant

Now if you obey me fully and keep my covenant, then out of all nations you will be my treasured possession.

Chapter 19 describes a momentous and terrifying meeting with God. Three months ago the people of Israel had been slaves in Egypt. During those months they had been led by Moses out of a life of ill-treatment and slave labour, seeing many miracles as God delivered them. Now they stand in the desert, before the mountain we call Sinai, waiting to hear what God through Moses will say to them.

We don't experience many solemn moments like this. Signing on to join the army might be such a moment, when you sign the dotted line and promise to obey, whatever happens, keep all the rules, and accept the possibility of hardship, injury and death. But this covenant between God and his people is also surprisingly like a marriage. God reminds them that they now know what he is like; how he has rescued them, saved them from slavery, carried them on 'eagles' wings' (19:4), that they will be treasured by him, that he has chosen them out of all other nations to be his special people.

Committing ourselves to a covenant relationship with Jesus and promising to follow him for the rest of our lives in a way echoes the solemnity of signing a contract with the army, *and* making marriage promises. We do not know what battles we may have to fight, but we are his chosen and beloved bride and because we love him we will obey and follow.

These are not laws to be obeyed to win the love and approval of God. He has already loved and saved his people; these are to be obeyed out of love and commitment.

Nothing we can do (even keeping these Ten Commandments) can make him love us more, and nothing we can do (even breaking them all) can make him love us less. His undeserved loving kindness that we call grace overwhelms us and in response we will do what pleases him.

MK

No other gods

He is the firstborn Son, who was raised from death, in order that he alone might have the first place in all things. For it was by God's own decision that the Son has in himself the full nature of God.

'I am the Lord your God. You shall have no other gods before me.' It is almost as if God is saying, 'I will reveal myself to you and then you will love and worship me and me alone.' Human beings cannot really know God or find out anything about him unless he shows himself to us. We can perhaps guess that he is mighty and creative by looking at the world around us. But we cannot know his love, his gentleness, his grace, mercy and forgiveness, his patience with us, his fatherhood, unless he tells us. The people of Israel knew God's love and care as he brought them out of slavery, but we know Jesus, the Son who has in himself the full nature of God.

This is the most amazing truth there is—the God who made the universe, who created everything we know, who made me and you, is shown to us in the man, Jesus Christ. We can read his words, listen to what he did, and we can fall in love with him, a man who knows what it is like to be human, and at the same time is the Lord God almighty, the creator. 'You shall have no other gods but me' is no longer the thunder on the mountain, but an invitation to a relationship as exclusive as the best of marriages, and as loving and intimate. We cannot betray him, turn to anyone or anything else because we are lost in love and adoration for the one who has loved us all the way to death.

I love you, Jesus. I will serve you and no other, for you are my God and there are no other gods.

MK

Do not make idols

Although they knew God, they neither glorified him as God nor gave thanks to him… They exchanged the truth of God for a lie, and worshipped and served created things rather than the Creator.

Paul's description of idolatry from his letter to the Romans helps us to make sense of one of the more difficult commandments. Of course we don't make idols—we have seen pictures on television of people bowing down to statues and carvings and we know we don't do that. But are there other ways to worship idols? There is a lot about idolatry in the Bible and mostly God is speaking to those who already know him, but still honour, or even worship, things that are not God. Are there things that are so important that we would serve them rather than God?

I have known someone who was so obsessed with having a clean and tidy house that she actually resented it when her family took books off the shelves, read the paper and left it on the coffee table, disturbed the fruit bowl by eating an apple or had a wonderful time with messy games. She had made the shell of their lives more important than their living. Can we do this with God? Valuing the way things are done in church rather than the worship itself? Following a church leader rather than the God he is teaching us about? Knowing God, but not caring to find out more about him? Nor joining with other believers in worship and prayer? Are we serving created things, even our own comfort, rather than the creator? Is God hidden from us by all the busyness, obsessions and little importances that we value so much?

It is very hard to see our own 'idols'. Sometimes it is only as we share and pray with a few trusted friends that we begin to see where we are not putting God first.

MK

Do not misuse the name of the Lord

How much more severely do you think those deserve to be
punished who have trampled the Son of God under foot, who
have treated as an unholy thing the blood of the covenant that
sanctified him, and who have insulted the Spirit of grace?

I work in central London, so every Christmas I watch the big
stores decorate their windows, and see the lights of Oxford
Street come on. We all grumble about aspects of Christmas, the
commercialism, the encouragement to buy, especially expensive
presents for children. We can see that much of the razzmatazz of
Christmas hides and distorts the real meaning of God becoming
a baby human being and then experiencing human life with
all its hardships and troubles. But what about my grandson's
infant school nativity play in which he played the part of a
snowflake and the main storyline involved a lost kitten, whose
mother searched everywhere and then in the end found her
kitten beside the manger? Does that distort the real meaning of
Christmas?

The trouble is that I am beginning to think that this command
is not about casual 'building site' blasphemy, however distasteful
that may be. It is about believers who know the *name* of God (that
is, they know him personally and understand his character), who
then misuse his name, distort the truth about him, make belief in
God and even God himself sound trivial. Perhaps our songs of
worship are sometimes just too light and casual. Sometimes we
sell Jesus to people as if he is a new kind of comfort blanket that
will make them feel better. Read the verse from Hebrews at the
top of the page again. How often do our church services convey
the awesomeness of God, his splendour, his consuming fire? Do we
misuse his name?

Name him, Christians, name him, with love strong as death,
but with awe and wonder, and with bated breath;
he is God the saviour, he is Christ the Lord,
ever to be worshipped, trusted and adored.
CAROLINE M. NOEL (1817–77)

MK

Remember the sabbath day

Looking for a reason to accuse Jesus, they asked him, 'Is it lawful to heal on the sabbath?' He said to them, 'If any of you has a sheep and it falls into a pit on the sabbath, will you not take hold of it and lift it out?'

Jesus had problems with people who remembered the sabbath day by keeping a great number of rules, even if that meant being unkind and unloving. Today most of us have problems with making one day in seven any different from all the rest! These are the kinds of changes in society that make knowing how to keep some of the commandments very difficult.

The command suggests that there should be a rhythm about work; that regularly we should stop, have a rest and some re-creation, take a breath before we start again. Many people are under such pressure and stress at work that this would seem to be very good advice. The command also suggests that we, particularly if we are employers, should take some responsibility for those around us, who won't be able to have some rest unless we allow them to.

To keep this command may require us to take stock of how our lives work out at the moment. Do you give enough time for simply sitting around, playing with the children, going for walks with friends? When someone gets a video to watch, do you sit down and watch it with them, or do you take the opportunity to tidy up, wash up, clear up?

But the sabbath commandment is not just about rest, it is also about keeping some time holy. We may not be able to rest on Sunday, the 'new' sabbath, which replaced the Jewish Saturday sabbath, or keep it holy in the ways we would like, but we can still build into our lives and the lives of those around us time to reflect, time to rest and time to look back and above all time with God.

Be honest with yourself: do you manage to make time to rest, reflect and pray?

MK

Honour your father and mother

'Who are my mother and my brothers? … Whoever does God's will is my brother and sister and mother.'

A rather successful church youth group had attracted a number of young people from non-churchgoing homes. One girl of 15 was in some distress because her parents had forbidden her to go to the group or to church. They regarded it as some kind of sect or cult, brainwashing the young and teaching them a lot of fairy tales. Should she withdraw and do what they ask, or does she have the right to disobey?

This command is not addressed to children—all of the commandments were addressed to adults, although, of course, children were included in the family and would be taught these commands by their parents. But it is about honouring and respecting our parents.

In the agricultural kin-based society of the Old Testament, parents, particularly fathers, controlled work, provided housing, educated and trained and arranged marriages for their children. So sometimes the command has been extended to include anyone in authority, in school, in the workplace, in government. We should always honour those 'above' us. But does this mean we should always do what they say and obey them?

In this story from Mark's Gospel, Jesus' mother comes to talk to him. It is clear from other passages that she does not understand his mission. He does not respond to her, but says that the family of faith, the fellowship of those who are disciples, is a closer relationship in some ways than our close family. Obeying God may mean sometimes that although we may still respect our parents, or others in authority, we may have to disobey them.

Honouring our parents means keeping in touch, including them in our lives, making sure they are looked after as they get older. It does not mean agreeing with them or even bringing up our children in the way they brought us up. We have to provide our children with the freedom to honour and respect us, but also sometimes to go their own way.

MK

Do not murder

'You have heard that it was said to the people long ago, "Do not murder, and anyone who murders will be subject to judgment." But I tell you that anyone who is angry with a brother or sister will be subject to judgment.'

Yesterday a friend in great distress told me that her son-in-law had left her daughter and their two small children for someone else. Her greatest emotion was one of enormous anger. How could anyone cause their own children such distress and misery and possibly spoil their chances of living a fulfilled and happy life? She wanted to express her anger in words and, if she had been stronger, in blows. Is that the kind of anger Jesus is talking about?

I knew two sisters once: the older one had a good job, was married with successful children; the younger one had never found a job she enjoyed and was always looking for something new. She was consumed with anger because she felt somehow that her sister's good fortune was unfair. This anger had spoilt her life. How far is that the kind of anger Jesus is talking about?

This command raises issues about killing human beings—in war, for example, or judicially by capital punishment—but it also requires us to look at our own lives and ask whether the Lord is pointing out something we should be dealing with. How much anger is there in you? Is it 'righteous' anger about a real injustice? Then maybe you should find out more about the injustice and even take some action. Is it anger against someone else that is eating your heart? Then you may need to confess and forgive. Are you aware of someone else's anger against you? Then again you may need to sort it out with them, even if you feel they are being unfair.

Anger can destroy us and be a form of murder. Or, in love, it can galvanize us into action to change ourselves and the situation.

Dear Lord, help me to deal properly with any anger in my life.

MK

Do not commit adultery

I tell you that anyone who looks at a woman lustfully has already committed adultery with her in his heart. If your right eye causes you to sin, gouge it out and throw it away.

Jesus extends the meaning of this commandment to include sexual longing for someone who is not ours. Watch one evening of television and count how many people are in sexual relationships with someone who is not theirs, let alone just looking and longing. It is a very popular plot for all kinds of drama.

I expect that many of the people reading these notes have been affected in some way by the betrayal and breaking of trust that comes with adultery. There are those who spend much of their lives with bitter regrets about an action that now seems so unimportant and brief, but has brought consequences, spoiling the lives of the people they really love—partners, parents, children, friends. Others may be in a marriage that is difficult and loveless. The temptation to find love elsewhere can be enormous.

Verses 29 and 30 in our reading are very strong language and very challenging. They are a measure of the catastrophic seriousness of adultery. Jesus is using graphic picture language to tell us we should avoid temptation at all cost; some have to fight this battle over alcohol, and some with sex and 'romance'. If we have a weakness, we cannot just do what others do; we have a special battle of our own.

But the gospel of Jesus is about repentance and forgiveness. There is no situation that cannot receive the balm of his love and grace. We all live with limits, handicaps, that we wish were not there; physical disability, failing exams, not being able to have our own children, never finding the right person to marry, spoiling the relationship that really mattered. In Jesus we learn to forgive and accept forgiveness, put things right as far as we can, accept the place and relationships we are in, and live to the full for him, within the limits that have been set for us.

MK

Do not steal

*'One thing you lack,' [Jesus] said. 'Go, sell everything you
have and give to the poor, and you will have treasure in
heaven. Then come, follow me.'*

An attractive, rich young man comes to Jesus. He wants to be
the very best for God and earn his place in heaven and asks Jesus
how he should do this. Jesus suggests to him that he already
knows the commandments and reminds him of some of them.
The young man claims that he has kept them since he was a boy.
The story then says that Jesus looked at him and loved him, but
also gave him the instructions in our verse. Why did he add
something so radical to the commandments?

One of the commandments Jesus listed was 'Do not steal'.
The young man was convinced that he had never stolen. But if
he was rich in a poor society, could that be wholly true? What is
stealing? Does it simply mean taking something that does not
belong to us or can we steal in other ways?

There were devout Christians who were slave-owners in the
eighteenth century. They would say that they never stole anything. But they took away people's lives, freedom, choices, right
to education, to paid employment, to stable family life. Wasn't
that stealing? The rich young man who came to Jesus was rich in
a poor land, where many were close to starving and widows were
often destitute. Are there other ways we can steal, apart from
simply taking something with someone else's name on it?

The rich have to ask themselves some very serious questions
about what it means not to steal. The commandments are for the
community of God's people, not just for the secret conscience of
the individual and maybe we are bound not just to keep them,
but to make sure that we do not make it more difficult for others
to keep them.

*The other side of stealing is generosity. Help me, Lord, not to worry
about who steals from me, but to be generous with what you have
given me.*

MK

Do not give false testimony

Do not pervert justice; do not show partiality to the poor or favouritism to the great, but judge your neighbour fairly. Do not go about spreading slander.

What happens when law breaks down, when you cannot trust witnesses, when the police plant evidence to get false convictions, when neighbours can covertly accuse each other to the secret police and have whole families imprisoned? Over the past ten years we have seen on the news terrible cases of injustice and false imprisonment. This commandment is about honesty in the courts; it is about perjury and false testimony.

Some people have suggested that the command is simply telling us not to lie. But I don't think it is as general as that. It is about saying things that hurt others, especially in the area of legal and judicial matters. There are many areas of life that come under this microscope: income tax returns, trade descriptions, secondhand car selling, political manifestos, advertising. If enough people give 'false testimony' in these areas, the judicial system and trade and finance, then the fabric of society begins to come apart around us. Being honest makes society work better, and brings comfort and well-being to our fellow citizens.

But for most of us the way in which we are most likely to disobey this commandment is in gossiping and slandering others. We repeat half-truths and rumours, or facts that are true but should not be repeated, and we too destroy reputations and damage relationships.

MK

Do not covet

'Do not set your heart on what you will eat or drink; do not worry about it… your Father knows that you need them. But seek his kingdom, and these things will be given to you as well.'

This is a commandment about our feelings and attitudes rather than our actions. Exodus 20:17 tells us not to wish we had our neighbour's belongings. Jesus tells us not to worry about what we will eat, or what we will wear. Human beings can waste their precious lives, hoarding and scheming, worrying and coveting.

It is perfectly reasonable to admire and appreciate things that belong to others, whether it is a lovely garden, a beautiful singing voice, or even success and achievement. We can usually tell when such admiration has turned into covetousness that begins to poison a relationship.

There are examples in the Bible of the terrible consequences of uncontrolled coveting. King Ahab wanted Naboth's vineyard and he ended up breaking commandments five, six, eight and nine. King David coveted Bathsheba, another man's wife. He broke commandments six, seven and eight. By breaking those, they were, of course, breaking the first—their commitment to worship and serve the Lord their God.

It is hard sometimes to live with little, next to people who have a lot. But this law reminds us that we must not let our cravings master us, that we are not entitled to possess everything we want, and that we are called to give up status and the admiration of others, not to seek it. Jesus tells us that if only we change the way we think, change our priorities, then our worrying and coveting will fade. There is an old chorus that goes,

> Count your blessings, name them one by one,
> Count your blessings, see what God has done.
> Count your blessings, name them one by one
> And it will surprise you what the Lord has done.

Are you able to change the way you count? It may surprise you. Seek his kingdom first and all these (other) things will be yours as well.

MK

The two greatest commandments

'Love the Lord your God with all your heart and with all your soul and with all your mind... Love your neighbour as yourself.'

Some experts in the law were disturbed by Jesus' teaching. He seemed to undermine the law or develop it further, as we saw in the commands about murder and adultery. He suggested that they misunderstood some of the laws, particularly the one about keeping the sabbath day. So they set out to test Jesus, asking him to name the greatest commandment in the law. In reply, Jesus did not name any of the Ten Commandments, not even the first one. He took two verses from other parts of the Old Testament; one about loving God, from Deuteronomy 6:4–5, and the other about loving neighbours, from Leviticus 19:18.

Jesus put love at the centre of being good; love at the centre of doing right; love as more important than duty. God is not an exasperated headmaster insisting on petty rules. He is not an angry father who sets down laws that we cannot obey and then punishes us. He is not demanding that we fulfil a list of conditions before he will let us into his heaven. These are not the steps we have to climb in order to find salvation. And yet many of the things people say about God and about Christian standards sound as if this is how they understand them.

Jesus says the first command is that we love God passionately, intelligently, deliberately, with our whole being. And we love him like that because Jesus has shown us what his love is like, the love that searched for us, found us, died for us and saved us, long before we even began to understand what loving meant. Safe and secure in that love, we then begin the magnificent adventure of loving our neighbours as ourselves. And who is our neighbour? Jesus answered that one too in the story of the good Samaritan. Everyone is our neighbour, and those we despise and find hard to love may be more loving neighbours than we are.

MK

Search, test, lead

Search me, O God, and know my heart; test me and know my anxious thoughts. See if there is any offensive way in me, and lead me in the way everlasting.

Love the Lord your God:

- Am I committed to him alone for the rest of my life?
- Is there anything else more important to me than my faith in Jesus?
- Do I deny him or use his name flippantly or trivially?
- Do I make time to be with him and pray to him?

Love your neighbour:

- Do I build honour and respect as well as love into my family relationships?
- Do I allow anger to drive me?
- Do I take risks with my marriage, or with the marriages of others?
- Am I keeping what I have even though others are in need?
- Have I damaged other people's lives by gossip?
- Am I honest in business and financial matters?
- Do I long for things that belong to others?

Thanks be to you, O Lord Jesus Christ, for all the benefits which you have given me, for all the pains and insults you have borne for me. O most merciful Redeemer, friend and brother, may I know you more clearly, love you more dearly and follow you more nearly day by day, now and for ever more. Amen.

RICHARD OF CHICHESTER

MK

Old yet ever new

The Lord is my shepherd, I shall not be in want.

This psalm is the most recited and the best loved. Even though the words may be familiar they still have the capacity to move, to challenge and to comfort. It is full of intimate detail and reads as a conversation between David and his loving Lord. Just recently, when I read this psalm again, I made it into my prayer, my conversation with him.

'Dear Father, because you are the shepherd of my soul I have everything I need, I lack nothing. You enable me to stop, even though the effort of doing so is harder than keeping going. But you have a place of safety and comfort for me where quiet waters flow and nothing hurries me or drowns out your still small voice. It is there that you restore my aching soul and heal my damaged body.

'And even if the way ahead is through the darkest of valleys nothing will frighten me for you will be with me just as you said, and even though all seems harsh and unyielding, comfort will come.

'You have lavished your provision upon me even in the most difficult of times. I am overwhelmed by your love and my life knows blessing upon blessing.

'Because of your grace I am pursued by goodness and love— they are my constant companions and will abide and remain with me all the days of my life.

'And as if this weren't enough, I will be where you are—at home in heaven, for ever. Amen.'

The familiar words of the Bible can transform our lives daily. The words are as relevant, as challenging as when they were first spoken because they were spoken to and by people just like you and me who faced the same situations we face. His words may be old, but they remain ever new!

Father God, may your word be real and relevant, challenging and comforting. May it find a place in our hearts and be lived out in our lives. Amen.

SW

Hebrews 12:1 (LB)

Go for it!

Since we have such a huge crowd of men of faith watching us from the grandstands...

The 'huge crowd' refers to those commended for their great faith in chapter 11. What a wonderful picture of a grandstand inhabited by the likes of Enoch, Noah, Abraham, Jacob, Joseph, Moses and countless others cheering us along in the race marked out for us!

The experiences and examples of the saints of old are in the pages of the Bible to encourage us along. But what of today? Do we have those around us to cheer us along? Are we part of a crowd or 'cloud of witnesses', as in the NIV version, cheering others along?

Regardless of our ability, we still have a part to play in others' lives. My days of participating in sports or most other activities are long gone. I spectate rather than participate. Initially it was difficult to be still and to watch. But the Lord reminded me of the words he spoke to the disciples: 'Watch and pray.' I could pray. I could cheer them along as I 'watched' their lives.

There is a story of a little boy who auditioned for a part in the school play. On the day the parts were awarded his mum went to collect him, fearful that he would be disappointed at not being chosen again. As she neared the school he rushed out to meet her. Wide-eyed with excitement, he exclaimed, 'Mum, Mum! I've been chosen to clap and cheer!'

As I pray for friends, perhaps in some small way I can 'clap and cheer' them along. I can join with others in forming our own 'cloud of witnesses' to pray, to clap and to cheer.

We all have a part to play—it isn't dependent upon our ability, only our availability.

Father God, help us to watch and pray, to clap and cheer for those around us and to play our part in each life. Amen.

SW

Here and now

Now faith is the substance of things hoped for, the evidence of things not seen.

Society seems to be inhabited by 'now' people. Yesterday is gone; tomorrow may not even dawn; all we have is the 'now'.

Recently I was phoned by a young friend asking if he could visit me. As I reached for my diary he quickly said, 'I'm here now! I'm on your doorstep.' The wonders of mobile phones!

Sometimes I simply cannot keep up with the 'now' generation. My life may not be able to keep up, but my faith can. I love the idea of changing the emphasis on the way we say these words. Try it: '*Now* faith…' What about now faith?

Now faith is as new and exciting as the first day it dawned upon us.

Now faith is fresh and new each day, like manna from heaven.

Now faith gives life substance as it focuses on God.

Now faith helps us to trust in the evidence of the things we cannot see. At times there seems little evidence that God is at work in our lives, unlike the days when he dwelt among us— wherever he went there was evidence that he had passed by! People were healed of every kind of disease and disability. Today, what evidence do we have? What evidence do we need?

Sometimes the biggest challenge we may ever face is to trust him; to trust that he is still with us, working in and through us, despite there being no outward evidence. Dare we? My answer is a resounding 'Yes!' I have all the 'evidence' I need: an empty tomb and a risen Lord is all that I need, to know that he is alive and that the faith that I have in him enables me to face every 'now' and every new day with all its challenges and opportunities.

Dear Father, help us to see that 'now' faith is the substance of things hoped for, the evidence of things not seen—yet! Amen.

SW

The plea of the helpless

Three times I pleaded with the Lord to take it away from me.

Paul was in good company—Jesus prayed three times in the garden of Gethsemane for the 'cup' to be taken from him. We don't really know what Paul's 'thorn in the flesh' was. But it drove him to plead with the Lord three times to take it away. I have lost count of the times I've pleaded with the Lord to take the MS away—it seems more like three hundred or three thousand times! But just as Paul received his answer and Jesus received the strength he needed, we too can know something of the sufficiency of his grace to help us and to hold us through the most difficult and horrid of times—and to understand something of the paradox of his strength being made perfect in our weakness.

Many things in our Christian lives are topsy-turvy and yet can reveal something wonderful about his grace. The list is intriguing and challenging. As A.W. Tozer said, 'We are strongest when we are at our weakest and weakest when we feel strong. We are often at our highest when we feel at our lowest. We can often do more by doing nothing and can go furthest while standing still. We have more when we have given all that we have away and have the least when we "possess" the most' (*The Best of Tozer*, Christian Publications Inc., 1978).

Only the Lord can make sense out of some of the things we face. Only he can turn our weaknesses into something useful, something worthwhile. We fear weakness and illness and having to depend on others. Yet even weakness, illness and dependency can be turned around for good if we allow his grace to flow through our lives.

Father God, your grace is indeed sufficient in all of our needs. Help us to know your strength even in our weakness. Help us to see the wonder of the paradox of trusting you. Amen.

SW

The harbour of acceptance

He replied… 'Shall we accept good from God, and not trouble?'

This question has taxed minds for centuries—how can we accept what often seems totally out of keeping with God's character and love? We are comfortable with good, but what about the hard times?

Some years ago, as I was tussling with the loss of function in my legs and the realization that I may soon need to use a wheelchair, someone used the term 'harbour of acceptance'. I had never heard of such a thing, but began to be drawn towards learning this most wonderful of lessons.

I had been in London as part of my job and had struggled all day long to get around. Now safely back on the train I began my journey home. I let my mind wander and remembered how I used to be—active, involved in everything. I was afloat on the high seas of life and enjoying every moment, even when things were rough. I loved it. I loved life! But now it was time for me to head into calmer waters, back to the 'harbour' where I could take stock of all that had happened over recent months: the diagnosis of MS, the changes physically. Once there, it seemed as if it was time to bid farewell to legs that functioned as I wanted them to; to a body that worked normally, properly. I closed my eyes and imagined myself on the harbour wall. From there I waved farewell to the life I loved, to the function I had, and began the process of acceptance, of being willing to accept this 'new' way of doing things.

I had no idea what lay ahead of me, only that in those brief moments on a train journey home I was facing a different sort of journey into a life I could never have imagined—but with the sure knowledge that the Lord would be with me and would keep me safe.

Dear Father, when we face those things we find difficult to understand, draw us into that safe place where acceptance comes. Amen.
                                                                SW

Dry bones

*He asked me, 'Son of man, can these bones live?' I said, 'O
Sovereign Lord, you alone know.'*

I cannot be the only one who has had hopes and dreams that
have died and become almost like this valley of dry bones Ezekiel
saw in the vision. He saw the nation of Israel rise up again and
become a vast army. Some of our hopes and dreams can come to
life again, have new life breathed into them, as God once again
begins to move on our behalf.

Jesus spoke about a seed falling to the ground and dying so
that new life could come. His death brought us life. It is a paradox of the Christian walk that from death can come life; from a
seemingly impossible situation can come something good .

Sometimes when I look at my life it seems as if the hopes and
dreams I had—to marry, to have children, to be healthy and
active—lie before me like dry bones, lifeless. Yet somehow and in
some way God has effected a change in my attitude to the loss of
my job, my home, and friends who could no longer cope with all
that was happening to me. Ability has been replaced by disability
and the 'death' of so many things, but as Jim Elliot said, 'We lose
what we cannot keep, to gain what we cannot lose' (Elisabeth
Elliot, *Shadow of the Almighty*, STL Books). At times things aren't
quite how we would want them to be—but whatever lies at your
feet today as dry old bones can be revived, can even be changed
into something altogether different. Just as the bones became
flesh and sinew, hopes and dreams can be transformed and can
turn out to be far better than we ever dared imagine.

*Dear Father, may your breath gently blow over our lives. Let us allow
you to revive, regenerate, renew our hopes and dreams. 'Can these
bones live? O Sovereign Lord, you alone know.' Amen.*

SW

To know him

Now this is eternal life: that they may know you, the only true God, and Jesus Christ, whom you have sent.

I became a Christian when I was eleven years old. I was intrigued and mystified by the concept of 'eternal life'. Some years earlier I had made the horrifying discovery that people die—a young friend had drowned in a local stream and for the first time in my life I realized that people don't last for ever. So when I met Jesus and heard about eternal life through him, I grabbed him—and it—with both hands.

As the years passed, my concept of eternal life changed—it isn't only the life that awaits me in heaven but a life to be lived here. Eternal life began that day I met Jesus, and is a lifelong journey into knowing him.

It seems all too easy these days to create a God in our image, a loving, kind God who wouldn't dare declare war on our concept of him. We can often allow our intellect to create a God who is very intelligent and reasonable; who is very scriptural and wonderfully easy to put in a 'box' and who complies to all our wishes and awaits our hurried prayers; a God who wouldn't allow illness and loss to come our way.

Eternal life is purely and simply *knowing him*—knowing him in the wonder of life, in the joys and the delights it brings. But it is, more importantly, knowing him when we have nothing to base that knowledge upon except the faith that comes from him alone, that holds us and sustains through the darkest of times.

But what matters supremely is that *he knows us*! We are graven on the palms of his hands, we are never out of his mind. His is the initiative, ours the response. We know him because he first knew us and continues to know us—as friends!

Dear Father, thank you for my eternal home in heaven. Help me to enjoy eternal life knowing you here and now, day by day. Amen.

SW

A sign of new life

*The Lord told [Ananias], 'Go to the house of Judas on
Straight Street, and ask for a man from Tarsus named Saul,
for he is praying. In a vision he has seen a man named
Ananias come and place his hands on him to restore his sight.'*

Saul, the Pharisee, of pure Hebrew ancestry; Saul, the impeccable
adherent of legalistic righteousness; Saul, the zealous persecutor
of the Christians. His reputation had gone ahead of him to
Damascus. It is no wonder, as we read this story, that we find
Ananias, an ordinary Christian disciple, exceedingly wary of obeying God's call to seek out this dedicated tormentor. But on his
journey to Damascus, intent on hounding the Christians, Saul
had an overwhelming vision of meeting the risen Jesus. And in
that meeting he was changed. Saul, the ardent opponent of Jesus
Christ became instead his humble, devoted follower.

Saul was temporarily blinded by his vision, and for three days
he fasted. What did he do during those days? He prayed. This
descendant of Abraham had taken his full part in all the Jewish
rituals, in the sacrifices, in the worship. But now, Ananias was
told, 'He is praying'. For the first time in his life prayer was no
formality. He was discovering what it meant to talk with God
as Moses had done, 'as a man speaks with his friend' (Exodus
33:11). In the next two weeks we will learn from Saul/Paul's
example in prayer: prayer that was intimate and bold, prayer that
knew God's heart.

I don't pretend that I know how to pray as Paul did. But I do
know that when my relationship with God changed from dutiful
churchgoer to heart-committed Christian, when I found new life
in Jesus, I really began to pray. Instead of merely repeating words
to a faraway, unknown being, I began to talk with a person who
was real and alive. 'He is praying.' That was the mark of Saul's
new life as a Christ-man.

*A question: Do you have the freedom in talking with God that comes
from having met Jesus?*

RG

In the family

You did not receive a spirit that makes you a slave again to fear, but you received the Spirit of sonship. And by him we cry, 'Abba, Father.' The Spirit himself testifies with our spirit that we are God's children.

Paul was sure that he was in God's family, not because of his ancestry, but because he had the Holy Spirit, the Spirit of Christ, in his heart. He put it even more clearly in writing to the Galatians: 'God sent the Spirit of his Son into our hearts, the Spirit who calls out, "Abba, Father"' (Galatians 4:6). Abba—the name Jesus himself used to address his heavenly Father. Isn't it amazing that we may, in fact are expected to, call God 'Abba' as Jesus did? What a privilege for us to be called God's children, to be counted in his family!

The New Testament has different images of the way we come to belong in the Father's family. One is that of adoption. One Son in God's family is unique; his place is his right, by his divinity. All the rest of us are adopted sons and daughters. But, just like the families on earth where the adopted children share fully the privileges of the natural-born children, God treats us fully as his children—with the privileges and responsibilities that go with belonging. Another New Testament image is that of being 'born again through the Spirit'. We acquire new natures, born again into God's family. Both images are biblical; it doesn't matter which appeals to us more. What matters is that we have the assurance that we belong in the family, that we can call God 'Daddy', a father who loves us, a father we know we can trust.

For some people the name 'father' is not a happy one. There are human fathers who are abusive, distant, absent, uncaring in different ways. It can take time to believe that God is the loving, wise, approachable God whom you can trust, whom you can talk with as Jesus did.

Ask the gentle Spirit to change your perception and to give you new confidence in prayer.

RG

To know God's love

I pray that you, being rooted and established in love, may have power, together with all the saints, to grasp how wide and long and high and deep is the love of Christ, and to know this love that surpasses knowledge.

Paul's own prayer life sprang from his relationship with God and his relationship with other people. That comes through constantly as we look at his prayers. We thought yesterday about how he wants each of us to be sure of our individual relationship with the Father, to know that each one has a special place in the Father's heart. Now he puts that relationship in the context of the whole Christian family, and of the enormity of God's love. It was pointed out to me recently that when we pray for other people we most often pray for some aspect of their physical well-being. But when Paul prayed for other Christians it was primarily for their spiritual health and growth. Look at his two main requests in this prayer.

First, he prayed for the power of the Spirit of Christ to strengthen them from within.

Second, he prayed that they might grasp the hugeness of the Father's love. It makes me think of an enormous oak tree, whose roots go deep and wide underground to draw moisture and food, to give the tree stability. Then the tree can grow tall, solid and healthy; its branches spread in all directions, its leaves drawing nourishment from the sunlight. That is an image of a Christian who has grasped something of 'the love that surpasses knowledge'.

Pray for someone who is important to you in Paul's words: 'Father, I pray that out of your glorious riches you may strengthen .... with power through your Spirit in his/her inner being.' Continue to the end of Paul's prayer. Then pray for yourself, again using his words: 'I pray that I, being rooted and established in love, may have power, together with other Christians, to grasp how wide and long and high and deep is the love of Christ.' May your roots grow deep and your 'tree' grow tall.

RG

Praise in prison

About midnight Paul and Silas were praying and singing hymns to God, and the other prisoners were listening to them. Suddenly there was such a violent earthquake that the foundations of the prison were shaken. At once all the prison doors flew open, and everybody's chains came loose.

Paul and Silas were in a sticky position. Falsely accused, flogged and imprisoned, we might expect to find them bemoaning their plight. Instead we find them singing hymns! We cannot always thank God for the circumstances in which we find ourselves; but we *can* always praise him for who he is: a trustworthy, faithful God who is right there with us, with good plans for us—even if they are not always the plans we would have made for ourselves!

We usually think of praising God when times are good, when we feel joyful or excited. But our praise doesn't have to be confined to those times. I remember one Saturday afternoon, years ago; I was lying on the floor in tears of deep loneliness. My husband was abroad; my daughter was away for the weekend; an important friendship had recently broken. And Saturday afternoon is not a time you want to disturb friends with a miserable SOS for help. Suddenly the floor was important! Just as the floorboards were supporting my whole weight, I realized that God was there, supporting me in my pain. I learnt a new dimension of praise that day, as I thanked God for his love and his presence. He changed my perspective even before he changed my circumstances.

For Paul and Silas, he changed their circumstances dramatically. An earthquake (an 'act of God', an insurance company would call it!) released all the prisoners. The missionaries did not use their freedom to escape, but to witness to the jailer and to help him to faith in Christ.

I will proclaim the name of the Lord. Oh, praise the greatness of our God! He is the Rock, his works are perfect, and all his ways are just. A faithful God who does no wrong, upright and just is he (Deuteronomy 32:3–4).

RG

Anxiety melted

Rejoice in the Lord always… Do not be anxious about anything, but in everything, by prayer and petition, with thanksgiving, present your requests to God.

Many years later, Paul was in another prison, in Rome, writing to the Christians in Philippi, where the church was now well established. The same note of joy and praise pervades. 'Rejoice in the Lord *always*.' Not necessarily rejoice in what is happening. But rejoice in a God who is faithful.

Of course, there is often an inner tug-of-war. There may be many things going on in your life at the moment to make you concerned, worried, anxious. In a small group last evening, there was a young woman with five children. She had surgery for a brain tumour six years ago, and told us of new problems with her eyesight. Is the tumour growing again? Not surprisingly, she is anxious. So how do we make the link between the God in whom we rejoice and the situation that can get us down? 'In everything,' says Paul, 'in *everything*, by prayer and petition [asking], with thanksgiving, present your requests to God.' He knows, of course, all that is happening in our lives. And he wants to help. But he wants us to come and talk to him, humbly yet confidently, knowing that he is trustworthy.

Sometimes we feel that we leave a time of prayer as burdened as we were when we started. A friend once spoke about 'butterflies with hobnailed boots' in her tummy! There is, actually, an element of choice. Without denying the strength of those butterflies I can choose to say to God, 'I know you are good. I know your resources are big enough for my situation. Please help me to trust you, because I want my trust to override my anxiety.' That doesn't ignore the fear; but it puts it in perspective.

And then, says Paul, you will know the peace that rises above normal human comprehension. The peace of God can be likened to the stillness of the ocean depths, untroubled by the waves on the surface. Lord, please help me to live in that peace.

RG

Not forgotten

I thank my God every time I remember you. In all my prayers for all of you, I always pray with joy because of your partnership in the gospel from the first day until now, being confident of this, that he who began a good work in you will carry it on to completion until the day of Christ Jesus.

'Out of sight, out of mind.' Could that be said of your prayers for your family members, your friends, the missionaries you know? I am afraid it is often true of me. Every December, we receive a large number of newsletters from friends worldwide, from recent acquaintances to friends of fifty years' standing. Many of them I forget from one year to the next. But those letters tell of joys and sorrows, of family needs, successes, uncertainties—all of them of interest to God. I often speed-read the letters… and then forget the people until next year.

Paul was not like that. 'I thank my God every time I remember you. In all my prayers for all of you…' I am constantly challenged by the dedication and consistency of this man who had planted scores of churches during the years of his itinerant ministry. He prayed for them all, without flagging. Three roots of his persistence stand out in the verses we have read today.

- **His good memories of their shared aim:** 'I always pray with joy because of your partnership in the gospel.'
- **His confidence in God's persistence:** 'He who began a good work in you will carry it on to completion.'
- **His deep love for them:** 'I have you in my heart… I long for all of you with the affection of Christ Jesus.' He prayed for them because he cared about them.

I am now going off to find a few of those December letters. As I reread them, I want to picture the friends, and allow God to highlight two or three items in each letter to help me to focus with thanksgiving and intercession.

Lord, please give me love for people and confidence in you that will join forces in sensitive, believing prayer.

RG

Praying for friends

This is my prayer: that your love may abound more and more in knowledge and depth of insight, so that you may be able to discern what is best and may be pure and blameless until the day of Christ.

So how does Paul pray for these Christians at Philippi whom he rarely sees but for whom he has such a deep affection? At first sight his prayer might seem to be a bit 'pie in the sky'. Is it that he doesn't know what is really going on in their lives? Oh no. Epaphroditus has brought both news (look at 2:25) and gifts (4:18). Paul is aware of men who want to undermine the gospel by insisting on Jewish practices (3:2) and he knows about the ongoing quarrel between two women in the church, Euodia and Syntyche (4:2). So let's look carefully at his prayer for them, a prayer that is in fact intensely practical, as he prays for a number of aspects of their lives. He asks:

- that their love may keep growing ('Euodia and Syntyche,' he might say, 'let love heal that quarrel').
- that love may be partnered by their knowledge of God and their spiritual insight (to recognize the false teaching).
- that they may be able to make the best choices in the way they live ('pure and blameless').
- for commitment to enable them to keep going 'until the day of Christ' (when Jesus will return in glory).

Think of some of the things going on in your own life: the joys, the sorrows, the struggles, the perplexities, the difficult relationships. Pray for yourself as Paul prayed for the Philippians. Then think of news you have received from friends in the last few days, in letters or phone calls, and pray for them, too. I think of a young woman, a very nominal Christian, who received news at 1.30 this morning that her father, a widower, had died of a sudden heart attack. Lord, I pray that in her grief she may find a new knowledge of you. And please give me insight to know how to talk with her when I next see her.

RG

God's special encouragement

One night the Lord spoke to Paul in a vision: 'Do not be afraid; keep on speaking, do not be silent. For I am with you, and no one is going to attack and harm you, because I have many people in this city.' So Paul stayed for a year and a half, teaching them the word of God.

Things were not always easy for Paul. His firm convictions and his passion for Jesus often stirred up opposition. When he arrived in Corinth he preached first, as he often did, to the Jews in the synagogue; when they opposed him, he continued to preach in the house next door! Many who heard him there were baptized, including the leader of the synagogue.

Such response must have encouraged him. How easily our moods rise or fall with the current circumstances. But I often find that, when everything seems to be against me, God gives a touch of encouragement. It may come from a change in the situation; through other people, in intentional kindness or a chance encounter; from a verse in the Bible, or direct from God himself. For Paul, God himself spoke. It is not clear whether Paul was awake praying or asleep dreaming. Jesus appeared and spoke to him, vividly. Such visions are not the staple diet of our lives (though talking with some Christians you might think they were!).

I am not a person who often gets pictures from God when I pray. But one occasion stands out to me. I was walking round a field, praying intensely about different aspects of a difficult situation. Suddenly, to my enormous surprise, I 'saw' a huge cross in front of me, almost disappearing in the clouds. Its size mattered; nothing was too big for him to forgive, or to help me to forgive those who had hurt me. Its height showed me the immensity of God's power to heal and to restore, and to enable me to withstand all that Satan might throw against me.

Lord, when I am discouraged, please show me yourself, your love and your power.

RG

Thankfulness

We always thank God... when we pray for you.

How do you start your prayers? It is easy to plunge in with saying sorry because we are feeling guilty, or by asking God for something because we are aware of a need. But Paul started either by praising a wonderful God, or with thanksgiving, because he was so aware of all the good things that God had done. It is the first thing we notice here: 'We always thank God'. And that word 'always' cropping up again is another reminder of how much he prayed. If I were to pray for a friend even once a month I wouldn't have the nerve to say 'always... when I pray for you'. Paul could say that—despite his long prayer list!

We need to read the rest of these verses to see what he was thankful for:

- 'Your faith in Christ Jesus'. That was the foundation of their life—and his.
- 'The love you have for all the saints'. He believed God's love so filled them that it overflowed in all directions. Can the same be said of you?
- 'The hope that is stored up for you in heaven'. Christian hope is not a wishy-washy 'it would be nice if it happens but I don't really think it will'. It carries a note of assurance: 'Yes, I expect it.' 'Stored up for you'—as if there is a deposit box in heaven with my name on it, to which my faith in Christ gives me the key. Our confidence is founded on 'the word of truth' which the Colossians had heard and grasped.
- 'The gospel [that] is bearing fruit and growing.' Paul rejoiced to see how the good news of Jesus spread, not only through him but through other Christians as they travelled throughout the Mediterranean world.
- 'Epaphras, our dear fellow servant'—faithful minister, messenger, friend.

Make a list of the good things God has done for you. Then thank him for each thing on your list, one by one.

                                                                    RG

A prayerful farewell

When he had said this, he knelt down with all of them and prayed. They all wept as they embraced him and kissed him.

So far we have focused on the 'spirituality' of Paul's prayers: his love for God, his passion for the gospel, his concern for the churches he had planted. Today his humanity comes to the fore as he says goodbye to his friends.

Near the end of a long missionary tour through Turkey and Greece, Paul was returning to Jerusalem by boat. *En route* he sent a message for the leaders of the thriving church at Ephesus to meet him at the nearby port. He reminded them of the example his lifestyle had set in the years he had lived with them, and he warned them against the church's enemies. It is a speech that all Christians, leaders in particular, would do well to read.

They were deeply grieved to know that this was probably their last meeting. But what a wonderful way to say goodbye! Where they were, on the beach I guess, they knelt to pray together. Do you ever pray with people for their immediate needs wherever you are, or do you wait until you are alone at home? A car park, a pavement, the phone, a restaurant, the car, even airport toilets are among the places I have prayed aloud with friends.

Paul and his friends were not only unashamed to pray in public; they were not afraid to show their emotions. Our prayers do not need to be so 'spiritual' that we avoid expressing our real feelings. Our fears, our sorrow, our anger can all be let out to God. As we tell him how we are feeling we can also ask him for trust, peace, joy and forgiveness to grow instead. It is noticeable in the Psalms how often the writer starts with an outburst of grief, pain, depression. Then we see a turning-point when he chooses to look upward, and the mood changes to joy and confidence. But our heavenly Father wants us to be real with him, not to show him an artificial smile.

Lord, thank you for all you show me through Paul's prayer.

RG

Strength for the battle

Our struggle is not against flesh and blood, but against the rulers, against the authorities, against the powers of this dark world and against the spiritual forces of evil in the heavenly realms... Pray in the Spirit on all occasions with all kinds of prayers and requests.

What does 'Ash Wednesday' convey to you? For some readers it means one of the most significant days in the Christian calendar. For others it means absolutely nothing! For me as a child it meant a boring, gloomy service in church—after the enjoyment of Shrove Tuesday's pancakes the day before! We link our church season of Lent with Jesus' forty days in the wilderness, when he battled with Satan. That is why I have chosen today's reading. Paul, like Jesus, was fully aware of the reality of Satan and his different methods of attack. So we can look on Lent as a time to pay special attention to the spiritual battle and our means to fight it. Here are three keys to victory:

Don't underestimate the Enemy. He's strong. He's invisible. He's crafty. He's dangerous. Our foe is not merely human, though the evidence of satanic activity is mostly seen in human behaviour. The unseen dark forces are real, powerful and deceptive.

Don't ignore your resources. Awareness of enemy strength does not mean that we have to cower in fear! Instead, we take stock of our defences. Our big resource is God himself—his strength, his gospel, his salvation, his word in the Bible, his reliability. He is a God we can actively trust. But our own character matters; we must live in truth and righteousness if we are to be able to resist a cunning enemy.

Keep in touch with your commander. You may think mobile phones are a boon or a bane! But they demonstrate the way God can catch our attention in out-of-the-way places, and we need to keep our 'spiritual phone' switched on at all times.

Writing this has helped me to make my own Lent resolution: Remember to talk with God wherever I am, whatever I'm doing. 'Pray... on all occasions.'

RG

To know him better

For this reason, since the day we heard about you, we have not stopped praying for you and asking God to fill you with the knowledge of his will through all spiritual wisdom and understanding.

From today till Saturday we are going to do things a bit differently. While the focus will change, I will ask you to read the same verses each day, and then to make Paul's prayer for the Colossians your own.

Here are Christians whom Paul had never met. Yet he was so moved by the news that Epaphras had brought that he prayed for them constantly. When I hear about a new Christian venture developing I can respond easily with, 'That sounds exciting. Lord, please guide and encourage them as they grow.' Then I forget. Paul wasn't like that. He didn't stop praying for them. He often challenges me with the consistency of his intercession. How can we take steps in the same direction? Maybe an organized prayer list will help: list some people you want to pray for daily, others weekly or monthly. Perhaps a ten-day rota would avoid the rut of 'Sunday services, Monday missionaries, Tuesday…'

Paul prayed first for their spiritual wisdom—that they might know God, and his perspective, better. We might say that he wanted them to have God's bird's-eye view of the world. We often pray for visible needs: if a friend is ill, we naturally want to pray for speedy recovery. It may well be right to do that. Paul did (Acts 28:6, for example). Do we also pray that the friend learns more about God through the illness? I know that I have learned more from God in the hard experiences of life than through the easy times. That is God's deep desire for us—to know him better. That was how Jesus prayed at the end of his life (John 17:1–26).

Make Paul's prayer in Colossians 1:9–14 a prayer for yourself. 'I ask you, God, to fill me with the knowledge of your will… I pray this in order that I may live a life worthy of you…' and so on.

     RG

To live like Jesus

We pray this in order that you may live a life worthy of the Lord and may please him in every way: bearing fruit in every good work, growing in the knowledge of God.

I have recently been reading *The Practice of the Presence of God*, the thoughts of Brother Lawrence, a 17th-century French monk. He was a man who 'lived a life worthy of the Lord', not because of the time he spent praying in the monastery chapel but because even in the kitchen where he worked for fifteen years ('to which he had naturally a great aversion') he set his mind on God. His love of God motivated him to 'do nothing, say nothing, and think nothing which may displease him', confident both in God's pardon for his sins and in receiving 'strength more than sufficient' when it was God's business he was doing. Old-fashioned language but a wonderful example for 21st-century Christians!

How do we translate this into the pressures of our own lives, where we are subject to the demands of families, employers, colleagues—let alone the demands we make of ourselves? We can start with the phrase we thought about yesterday: 'the knowledge of his will'. 'Lord, show me what *you* want me to do—or to leave aside—today.' We can be sure that we are talking to a God who understands about living under pressure. When Jesus lived on earth, there were constant demands on his time, his strength, his wisdom. His motto was, 'I do always those things that please him (his Father God)'. If we want to live like him, we must try to be like him, for what we are matters more than what we believe.

Use Paul's prayer to pray for people you know—friends, family members. 'I ask you, God, to fill .... with the knowledge of your will, that she may live a life worthy of you, and may please you.'

RG

Today is the Women's World Day of Prayer, and this year the theme is 'Informed Prayer—Prayerful Action'. The service has been prepared by ecumenical women of Samoa. Join with thousands of women praying today. The Bible readings are Esther 4:1–17 and Matthew 15:21–28.

MR

To grasp his power

Being strengthened with all power according to his glorious might so that you may have great endurance and patience, and joyfully giving thanks to the Father who has qualified you to share in the inheritance of the saints in the kingdom of light.

'Oh! I just haven't got enough energy! There's a pile of clothes waiting to be ironed—and at least six urgent letters to write… and Aunt Caroline's coming to stay on Sunday… and Jamie wants books from the library for his science project… and…'

What does Paul have to say to us as he prays for the Colossians? 'Strengthened with all power according to his glorious might.' That is not just for 'special' people. Each one of us is special to God! Elsewhere Paul writes about 'his incomparably great power for us who believe'; and he goes on to liken this power to God's 'mighty strength, which he exerted in Christ when he raised him from the dead and seated him at his right hand in the heavenly realms' (Ephesians 1:19–20). Wow! I confess to my own present tiredness, tempted to panic that I will be unable to do all the things that loom in front of me. Then I read that the power that raised Jesus from the dead is the power that is available to me. 'Lord, please give me peace and energy to do everything well and in order. Forgive me if I have undertaken more than I should, and I trust you to get me through this time. Thank you for your power, available for me today.'

We have used Paul's prayer to pray for ourselves, and for friends. Now use it to pray more widely, even for some who are total strangers to you: pray for church leaders, for missionaries, for emergency relief workers, for the medical profession, for people in the news. May those who ignore God at present come to a knowledge of his will; may they live lives worthy of their maker; may they have the strength for good things they seek to accomplish. Take Paul's thoughts, apply them, pray them.

Lord, may my small prayers help to make some difference in your world.

RG

Introducing Galatians

Paul's letter to the Galatians is dynamite—a real rocket of a letter. It has been called the 'great charter of Christian freedom', and gets off to a sizzling start. Paul is writing to address some urgent problems that have arisen in the churches, and he is so appalled that there is no room for politeness. Such is the passion of the letter that by the time they'd read it, most likely the Galatians were glad Paul had not visited them in person!

Galatia was a huge Roman province that stretched across the mountains and plains of central Turkey. On his first great missionary journey (Acts 13 and 14), Paul had visited the Galatians of the southern cities, and brought them the good news of salvation through Jesus Christ. They had heard him gladly and given him a warm welcome, although he was not well. Paul had stayed on to establish his young converts into communities of Christians in Antioch, Iconium, Lystra and Derbe.

But then he got news that other Jewish-Christian teachers had arrived in Galatia. Whereas Paul had taught that repentance and faith in Christ were all that was needed for God's forgiveness and new life, these teachers said no, not quite. They said that non-Jewish converts must be circumcised and observe the Jewish law in order to be righteous.

Paul was distraught, for this message attacked the very roots of the Christian gospel. Christianity taught that salvation was God's gift to all who believe in Christ. But this new teaching said that obedience to the law was just as essential as faith in Christ. Paul wanted to shout at the Galatians, to wake them up from this folly. To come to God through Christ, and then turn away and prefer to try and approach God through obedience to the law, was madness. It would be useless. There was only one gospel, only one way of salvation—through Christ.

Paul's letter to the Galatians was probably written about AD49.

Dial 999 and ask for heaven

…who gave himself for our sins to rescue us from the present evil age…

Ever noticed how popular 'how to succeed' books are? Once it was *How to Make Friends and Influence People*. Nowadays *feng shui* promises you all sorts of success if you can just sort out your furniture. But if, even after you have moved the couch, you still can't communicate with the man who is on it, reach for *Men are from Mars, Women are from Venus*, and that should do it.

In a success-oriented world, we are encouraged to take charge of our lives, to plan for success, to carefully accumulate money, position and prestige. But when it comes to the spiritual things of life, you cannot 'play to win'. Spiritual health is not achieved through workouts in a metaphysical gym. In fact, humiliating as it may be to modern men and women, we can do nothing to save ourselves.

We have been *rescued*… from *our sins*.

This must seem nonsensical to many people. They may admit to being morally challenged at times, but not sinful. As for being rescued, that implies helplessness, and your modern, success-oriented executive type is simply not programmed to think that they need to be rescued from anything—and certainly not their sins!

So how does one reach these sorts of people with the grace of God? Sin and rescue are meaningless ideas if you've just topped £40,000 a year and have a new Alfa Romeo to go with it.

One thing that might do it is 'the present evil age' itself—no one's life runs smoothly, and trouble can be what C.S. Lewis would call 'God's megaphone' to get people's attention. Because people in trouble know they need help.

If you know someone in this position, pray that you will have wisdom as you talk with them about spiritual things. If your friends are presently losing out in this world, tell them about the spiritual world, where they need not lose out. Gently point them towards the only one who can really rescue them.

AC

Eye of newt

I am astonished that you are so quickly deserting the one who called you... [for] a different gospel—which is really no gospel at all.

Have you ever read the James Herriot books? He worked as a vet from the 1930s onwards, a time when veterinary medicine was being transformed. Many of his stories involve farmers, bewildered at the new medicines, and wanting the old treatments back. Thus, when their cattle had sore throats, they wanted liniment to rub on the necks, and were dismissive of antibiotics in the shoulder. In another story, a dog with an underactive thyroid gland is losing all its hair. Frantically the owner rubs in smelly ointments, and he is confounded when James restores the coat with injections into the bloodstream. Again and again James has a frustrating time trying to convince the people of Darrowby that the new treatments are at last reaching what is *really* the matter with the animal, and not just dealing with the visible symptoms.

Paul faced something similar with the bemused Christians of Galatia and the Jewish-Christian teachers who'd descended on them. For centuries, the Jews had practised observance of the law. Now Christ had come. They had heard the message that Christ alone could give them access to God, but they did not believe it. The law they knew; and its treatments for various sins were always applied to the spot where trouble broke out.

But Paul knew that only Christ could cure what was really the matter with humankind—deal with the sin in the bloodstream, as it were. Law might keep the symptoms under some control; only he could put a new Spirit in men and women, and end the infection that would lead to death. After Christ, therefore, living by the law was irrelevant, a backwards step.

Try an experiment—if you have the nerve! Next time the doctor prescribes you antibiotics, tell him you'd much rather stick with the old ways your ancestors used—wing of bat and eye of newt... and see what reaction you get!
Read Romans 4 and 5.

AC

Time out

...immediately into Arabia...

What an extraordinary line! If you like stories with unexpected twists and turns, here is one. Paul has grown up steeped in Judaism, and has suddenly had a galvanizing vision of Christ. He knows at once that he is called by God to be an evangelist. So what happens next? Three alternatives seem obvious. He could:

- Go to Jerusalem to 'touch base' with Peter and other leaders, and devise a strategy for Church growth.

- Return to his old Jewish colleagues, and witness to them.

- Immediately go and set up a mission to the Gentiles.

Instead: 'I did not consult any man... nor did I go to Jerusalem... but I went immediately into Arabia...' No Christian churches. No Jewish friends. No evangelism. No sense?

But wait a little. Presumably, if Paul went to Arabia, it was because he knew that God wanted him to go. Alone. Far from his former life, from present Christian company, from the future work he was called to do.

Has something similar happened to you? After a time of great blessing, do you now feel isolated, among people who do not understand you? Don't be alarmed. Perhaps God wants you to be alone, to give you space to seek him. Perhaps even the great Paul needed time to separate himself from his old life, to get to know Christ in a deep, inner way, and to prepare for his future life.

So, if you are isolated and it seems as if you have lost everything dear to you, be patient. God is still with you, and perhaps he wants to prepare you for a new work. Sometimes our future is being prepared under our noses, and we don't see it. Paul had grown up in the thick of Jewry. Now he is alone in Arabia. But this was his future—to take the gospel to the Gentiles.

What new thing could God be seeking to do in your life? What hidden talents does he want to stir up in you?
Read Galatians 1:21–24.

AC

Not the White House

…they saw that I had been entrusted with the task of…

In last year's American presidential election, untold thousands of people worked themselves silly to help get their man into the White House. The new President had no idea who most of them were.

People also worked hard to get themselves into more prominent local positions. Democrats and Republicans across America rivalled each other for a bit more power at city and state level.

Not so in Christianity. Our leader does not need us to fight for him; he has fought for us. And he knows who each single one of us is. He does not want us to rival each other for work in his name either. He never offers two people the same job and leaves them to slug it out as to who'll get it. He calls us by name, and he sends us by name to do the work for which *we* were made. He does not want us to seek our own success and notoriety, but to serve his body on earth—out of love for him.

Why not spend some time soon thinking through what Christ has called *you* to do with your life? You may not be Paul or Peter, but that does not mean that the Lord has nothing special in mind for you. Here are some guidelines:

The gift will be already there within you. 1 Peter 4:10 urges, 'Each one should use whatever gift he has received to serve others.' Personalities are *used*, not overridden.

And note that the work will be that of *service*. If you want to be a famous, well-admired Christian who is quoted in the national press, beware your motives.

The work should not be that to rival any other Christian. God does not set us against each other. Ephesians 4:3 urges, 'Make every effort to keep the unity of the Spirit through the bond of peace.'

Paul and Peter knew exactly what they were about—and thus were enable to enjoy true fellowship with each other. What about you?

Read Galatians 2:9–10.

AC

Aslan and the White Witch

I have been crucified with Christ and I no longer live, but Christ lives in me.

There is a moving scene in *The Lion, the Witch and the Wardrobe* by C.S. Lewis, where Aslan the Lion offers himself as the victim to be killed by the White Witch in place of one of the children, Edmund, who is under sentence of death as a traitor.

The children are distraught. The forces of evil cackle with glee. At last they have the right to kill—the Deep Magic says traitors must die. That Aslan should offer himself instead of the guilty one overjoys them.

They close in on Aslan, bind him to the Stone Table, and cruelly beat him. The White Which shrieks in triumph to Aslan, 'Now I will kill you instead of him… but when you are dead, what will prevent me from killing him as well?'

So Aslan dies. But next morning, as Susan and Lucy weep, the field mice nibble his ropes away. Then suddenly the sun rises, and Aslan is alive in all his golden glory.

The White Witch is appalled, but has nothing left to fall back on. The Deep Magic has been fulfilled; a victim has died. She has done her worst, and it is not enough. She discovers too late that the Deep Magic had no power to hold an innocent victim. Aslan is alive again. The children are alive. Nothing can harm them now.

Paul must have felt like this. He suddenly realized that the law he had feared and respected all his life had caught up with him, and that the sentence of death had already been executed—but executed on the body of Christ on the cross. Paul's sins had caused death—but Christ had taken his place, and now he need never fear again. No wonder he writes, 'The life I live in the body, I live by faith in the Son of God, who loved me and gave himself for me' (Galatians 2:20).

Read Romans 7:4–6.

AC

Galatians 3:1–5 (NIV)

How to be perfect

After beginning with the Spirit, are you now trying to attain your goal by human effort?

Bishop Festo Kivengere of Uganda, an outstanding Christian leader in the days of Idi Amin, once shared something of his early struggles as a Christian: *'My problem was understandable: I wanted to leave sin completely behind. I reasoned: "Sin is against my Lord; he wants me to be perfect, so I must be perfect…"'*

But Festo's efforts didn't work, and he was miserable. *'Anything that smacked of having failed God, or falling into temptation, to my mind was just terrible!'* One night he began to pray in real despair. Midnight came and went. Suddenly, he felt as if the Lord quietly said to him, *'Festo, how did you come to me first?'*

'Oh, I was in bad shape, Lord.'

'And did you find me lacking to meet all your needs?'

'No, Lord, you did it in a minute. You filled my empty heart, you lifted the burden of my sin, you changed my hostility into love, you opened a whole new world to me. It was you alone, by the Holy Spirit, Lord. But what do I do now, Lord?'

'You have done everything you can to be perfect, but you have not turned your focus on me. As you first received me, so, in the same way, also walk. Where did you get your liberation?'

'At the cross.'

'Go there. Again and again.'

It was as if heaven opened that evening for Festo. He had wanted to find the key to perfection in order to please Jesus; but Jesus *was* the key. He had been looking for a solution other than Jesus. He had got to the position where he knew Jesus had saved him, but now Festo wanted the secret of being perfect so that he could please him.

That evening brought a breakthrough. *'I learned that God is sufficient for everything, and that a deeper relationship with Jesus was all I needed. All I had to do to be a successful Christian was to continually turn to Christ.'*

Read Ephesians 1:17–21.

AC

Equal opposites

There is neither Jew nor Greek, slave nor free, male nor female, for you are all one in Christ Jesus.

This verse was dynamite 2000 years ago. Paul may as well have said, 'Neither Martian nor Earthling', so wide was the gulf between these opposite groupings in first-century society. People were classified by religion, their status as citizen, and their gender. This was the first time anyone had ever thought of uniting the opposites *as equals* in any way, shape or form.

So what was Paul saying in this verse?

'Jew nor Greek': for centuries each had had their own way of reaching out to God. Paul says that this is now irrelevant; even Judaism has been superseded. For God has only one way of reaching out to humankind—all of them—through Christ.

Today, worldwide, there are Christian converts from all backgrounds: Hindu, Muslim, Jewish, pagan. It doesn't matter how they were trying to find God; *Christ found them*. If you've ever been to an international gathering of Christians, you'll have seen this wonderful unity.

'Slave nor free': here was earthly power at its most savage—who owns *you*? Slave had no rights, no possessions—they didn't even own themselves. But Paul says that God valued the slaves as much as the free. Hence the widespread Christian social concern over the centuries. Wherever people are enslaved by poverty or oppression, you will find Christians there labouring to help, because in Christ, they regard those people as equal—and deserving of equal rights.

'Male nor female': an ancient Jewish prayer ran, 'I thank you, O Lord, that I was not born a woman.' And those men meant it: women's lives were not to be envied. Down the centuries, this has often remained true. But God did not intend the sexes to oppress each other. In Ephesians (5:28) Paul says, 'Husbands ought to love their wives as their own bodies. He who loves his wife loves himself.'

Read Ephesians 4:1–16.

AC

Fathers and daughters

Because you are sons, God sent the Spirit of his Son into our hearts, the Spirit who calls out, 'Abba, Father.'

Abba is the Aramaic word for 'daddy', the familiar form of 'father'. In this verse, Paul tells us that we are not on formal 'father' terms with God. Because we have his Spirit within us, we are truly part of the family, and find ourselves on warm, loving terms with God: '*Abba*', 'Daddy'.

What relationship did you have with your earthly father as a child? Did he give you the loving support you needed? Could you trust him to take care of you? Fathers can be very critical of us as daughters. Our relationship with them can go on to affect our relationship with our husband and sons. It can also affect how we see God. Whether or not you have personal experience of what having an *abba* can be like, the Bible is full of examples of how your heavenly Father behaves. So, for example:

If your father was too busy for you when you were small, read Mark 10:13–16. Jesus said: 'Let the little children come to me.'

If your father was careless of things you needed when you were growing up, read Matthew 6:25–34: 'Do not worry… your heavenly father knows…'

If your father has condemned you for misspent money or living too wild, read Luke 15:11–32, the story of the prodigal son.

Or perhaps your father never cared enough to bother where you were, or what company you kept. Read Matthew 18:10–4, the story of the lost sheep.

If your father condemned your choice of boyfriends, read John 8:1–11, the story of the woman caught in adultery.

If you grew up with a father who never bothered to plan and save for your future, read John 14. Jesus has a place set aside in heaven for you.

And if your father was usually too busy with work or hobbies to spend time with you, read John 15—Jesus wants you to 'abide in him'.

Read Matthew 7:11.

AC

What's wrong?

What has happened… have I now become your enemy?

I once befriended a girl in the rain on the Isle of Cumbrae, west of Largs. We got chatting as we sheltered in a shop doorway, and when she discovered I was a Christian, she asked me to help her become one too—within twenty minutes of meeting! I was staying with some local Christians who could at least completely understand her Glaswegian accent, so I took her back to their house and they prayed with her. In the years that followed, we corresponded, and it was a sheer joy to learn of her joining a local church in Glasgow, and of growing in her faith.

I also once befriended a girl from the South Atlantic. She, too, was very interested in Christianity. When she moved to Bristol, I spent a day on the phone to find some Christians there for her. A doctor's wife agreed that this was God's task for her in the coming months—to befriend my friend. But things did not work out. Our South Atlantic friend began to demand things— endless time and outings. Then she got in trouble with the police. It was heartbreaking. The doctor's wife and I felt sad that our friend from the South Atlantic should reject what was good, and eventually slip away to an unwise lifestyle.

Here Paul is in real grief because the Galatians, whom he had 'fathered' in faith, were also slipping away. Did their past great kindness to him, his gratitude and the close friendship that had resulted mean nothing to them? 'Have I now become your enemy?'

Have you ever had a friendship wither? When you have been trying to encourage someone in spiritual matters as well, it hurts all the more when they reject you.

Take comfort in the fact that if it could happen to Paul, it can happen to any Christian, and understand his heart cry: 'How I wish I could be with you now… because I am perplexed about you!'

Read the last verse of Galatians, to see how Paul left the matter.

AC

Practical love

Love your neighbour as yourself.

This is a true story, but it could probably only happen in America. A family who had not been Christians for long moved to a new town, and decided to go to church on their first Sunday morning. They were given a warm welcome, and decided to attend evening service. They returned to find that their new home, with all their possessions—most still unpacked—had burned to the ground.

The pastor and his congregation, who had met them for the first time that morning, rallied round. Clothes were found, food was dug out of deep-freezers. One couple at the church was leaving on a three-week holiday—they handed over their house keys to the devastated family. By the time the insurance came through, and the family could begin to replace home, furniture and personal belongings, they had had time to do a lot of thinking, and they wanted to say some things to the congregation.

Although of course they were heartbroken to lose all their personal effects, they said that the love they had been shown by the Christians had made them realize for the first time something of what God's love must be for them. At no time had they felt abandoned or forsaken. The experience, dreadful though it had been, had at least helped them discover the spiritual reality of the body of Christ, and its loving care. The family felt they had grown in Christian maturity faster in those few weeks than they would have done otherwise in years.

The moral of this is not to go out and leave your gas fire on, hoping it will help your spiritual life. Nor is it to burn down your neighbour's house, if you think they are a bit dry spiritually! It is just to reflect that when we show practical, sacrificial love for our neighbours, it can be a powerful testimony to our faith. Such practical love is totally giving and non-threatening—it simply reflects Christ's love.

Read 1 John 3:17–20.

AC

Sin sells

...the acts of the sinful nature...

When did you last go to the cinema and watch the trailers for all the other films coming on? Did they seem a potent mix of some (or all!) of the following?

'Sexual immorality... debauchery, idolatry and witchcraft, hatred... jealousy, fits of rage, selfish ambition, dissensions, factions... envy, drunkenness, orgies...'

Sounds like the plot for a new hit film, based on life at the beginning of the 21st century—and the continuing meltdown of Western civilization.

A study of the rise and fall of successive empires shows a definite pattern, whether it be ancient Greece, ancient Rome, medieval Christendom, or modern England. History shows that empires rise as they turn away from religion, but then decline, because without the underpinning of religious belief, the morality that glues society together fades away.

In the West today, materialism has triumphed, and undeniably transformed our living standards. But our declining moral standards are at the same time destroying what has been achieved, for crime is everywhere, and our personal relationships (especially between the sexes) are turning sour. Sexual disease is on the increase; family life is on the decrease.

And if the words from Paul sound like a plot for a new film, is that a surprise? Our arts are turning increasingly to mindless, meaningless sensationalism, until violence and explicit sex unite in pornography. Martin Scorsese, describing his film 'Cape Fear' to the *Los Angeles Times*, listed its vicious beatings, attempted rapes, drowning, burning, and worse, and declared, 'It's a lot of fun.' His film is only one of hundreds of similarly violent films which are also thought by audiences across the world to be 'a lot of fun'.

Meanwhile despair and disgust run rampant in modern society. So we resort to pills to keep the panic and depression under control, and turn to suicide when we can't.

There is a better way. Read Colossians 3.

AC

Dig deep to be fruitful

But the fruit of the Spirit is love, joy, peace, patience, kindness, goodness, faithfulness, gentleness and self-control.

The list of today's qualities could not be more different than that of yesterday's. After the maelstrom of hatred and dissent, here is the ordered, sane world of the Spirit of God.

Of course, it is easy to love, be joyful, be at peace, be kind and all the rest when all is going well in your life. But what about the times when you are facing hostility, misery, constant irritation, evil, betrayal and even violence? All of us live our lives with a certain degree of unhappiness: how can the fruit of the Spirit flourish in such circumstances?

Perhaps the secret is in remembering how fruit is formed.

First, to be fruitful, a tree needs pruning. When the Spirit abides in us, 'every branch that does bear fruit he prunes'—not to hurt the tree, but so 'it will be even more fruitful' (John 15:2). But pruning can be painful; if not to trees, certainly to us.

Second, to be fruitful, a tree needs nourishment. The atmosphere of your daily life—at home or work—may be poisonous, stifling or bitter, but you don't have to inhale it. Instead, be like a tree—dig your private, inner roots deep into the ground of God's Spirit, and feed on him. It will give you an inner poise, a balance, a detachment from the things around you. Take refuge in God, and let his Spirit shield you.

The Psalms were written in a desert country, where plants exposed to the blistering sun died quickly without any refreshment. So the psalmist understood your problem. But Psalm 1 promises that anyone who turns to God will be able to defy the scalding vapours around them. They will be 'like a tree planted by streams of water, which yields its fruit in season'. So, let the dryness of your daily life spur you on to dig deeper into the boundless resources of the Spirit of God.

Read Psalm 1.

AC

You can't compare

If anyone thinks he is something when he is nothing, he deceives himself. Each one should test his own actions. Then he can take pride in himself, without comparing himself to somebody else.

How do you rate yourself? As a success or a failure? And what is your measuring line? Humans are social animals, so of course we take our 'measuring lines' from other people and their expectations. The pull to conform, to compete, is strong. But we need to be aware of some of the pitfalls involved.

Paul here begins by warning us to be on our guard against self-importance. Basically, if you don't really have it, don't flaunt it! You may deceive yourself, but not other people. My local leisure centre employed an extraordinary car park attendant who threatened to punch people in the face if they did not park where he told them to. People were not impressed, and he was sacked.

Paul instead urges us to aim for individual excellence. 'Then he can take pride in himself, without comparing himself to somebody else.' You know the famous line-portrait of one woman: 'It's not enough that she should succeed; all her friends must fail.' Sadly, many women are like this. Someone I know has a sister-in-law with four children. The sister-in-law was friendly during the years that this person was alone and hard up. Now she has a fiancé with money, and the sister-in-law hasn't been round for months. Why are some women so threatened by the success of others? Insecurities, jealousies... who knows?

But life is more than trying to shine brighter than everyone you meet. Because at the end of the day, marks will not be awarded on your success over other people.

God does not care whether you can do what other people are doing better than them, but whether you are doing what you are supposed to be doing, to the best of your ability.

What a marvellous release! Fancy being able to be satisfied with yourself, and having God's approval.

Read Proverbs 31:10–31.

AC

Spring flowering

Do not be deceived: God is not mocked. A man reaps what he sows.

What you plant grows. What you don't plant doesn't grow. I always think of the above verse in the spring, not autumn. It's because every spring, when I'm fed up with winter, my spirits get such a lift from all the crocuses and snowdrops and daffodils… in my neighbours' gardens. The few flowers that come up in my garden embarrass and enrage me—why, oh why, when I had the chance, didn't I put in more bulbs last autumn?

I guess it was because everything seemed so warm and pleasant and fruitful then. There were flowers everywhere. It was hard to realize and accept that coldness and darkness lay ahead… and beyond that, a time of new life, when I would be glad of having planted things that would blossom *after* the season of death.

Our deeds *here* will reap destruction—or eternal life—*there*. When we are alive in this world, with all its mellow fruitfulness around us, it can be hard to think that we won't always be here, and always free to do as we like. It's hard to imagine a time when we shall die, and when our lives will be held to divine account.

Perhaps all the material things in this life—prosperity, security, and so on—are like thriving annuals. They look wonderful, smell fantastic, give a great show, and make your garden look a real success. But when winter sets in, they wilt with the first frost, and when they die, that's it.

We know our gardens will be here next spring, and so we plant mostly perennials that will outlive the season of death. We allow space for just a sprinkling of annuals, for a bit of colour and fun, but we need to remember that they will not last for ever.

If we live to please the Spirit, we are sowing autumn bulbs. They do not bloom until after the season of death. If we live only to please ourselves, we are relying on annuals. And you can't take them with you.

Read Revelation 21:1–8.

AC

Lord of the dance

Does God supply you with the Spirit and work miracles among you by your doing the works of the law, or by your believing what you heard?

It was a throwaway remark at the beginning of the sermon—that the seemingly insignificant word translated 'supply' in this verse is *'epichoregon'* in Greek. The *chor* bit, from the same root as 'choreography', means 'dance', and the whole thing has to do with 'the one who arranges a dance for a village'. The preacher said, 'Isn't that lovely?' but didn't explore it further. I thought I'd like to do so here!

I discussed with a group of Christians the sort of dance we thought God might arrange. It wouldn't be ballet, we decided, which requires years of training for dancers and an audience which pays, applauds but otherwise just sits there. It wouldn't be 'Come Dancing', complete with judges and elaborate sequinned costumes, nor disco where people dance either by themselves or in a passionate clinch. No, it would be like a village barn dance. Anyone from children to OAPs can turn up in ordinary clothes. It doesn't matter about knowing the steps; anyone can join in, provided they're willing to get up on their feet, listen to the music and obey the caller. Give it a bit of energy and you'll have a ball—and make lots of friends!

The Christian way of life is not some rigid affair we're badgered into by law, nor the spiritual equivalent of impossible ballet exercises at the barre: God arranges the dance of life through his gift of faith, of miracles, of his Spirit, of himself. These may not arrive neatly to order—arranging a dance for a village takes time and involves our co-operation—but the Lord of the dance is in charge and supplies our joy as well as our need!

Help us to see beyond ourselves and to enjoy being part of your dance in the village in which you have set us.

CL

A feast at the dance!

He who supplies seed to the sower and bread for food will supply and multiply your seed for sowing and increase the harvest of your righteousness.

Guess what? That little word 'supplies' means 'arranging a dance for a village' again. For God does supply enough food for the whole global village of planet Earth to 'have a ball' every day—it's just that greed, hatred and other sins mean some people starve while others over-indulge.

Here Paul is asking the Corinthians to make ready their gift which will help prevent Christians in Jerusalem from starving during the predicted famine. But it's not just up to the efforts of that one church. God, who is choreographing the whole thing, will treat their contributions, together with those from other churches, like grains of wheat which will grow and multiply—and in the end enrich the giver as well as the recipient.

In the 1980s I saw a video about some ordinary Christians in Texas who found out that, just across the border, in Juarez, Mexico, people were living in poverty on a rubbish dump. They decided to take them some food on Christmas Day but were dismayed when far greater crowds turned up than expected. They asked God to bless the food, gave it out and experienced a 'loaves and fishes' miracle. The limited supply of food they had brought lasted until the final person was well fed.

It didn't end there. Over the years, God used them to bring not only food but work, dignity, justice and Jesus to those people, transforming the 'dance' of two communities, one American, the other Mexican. The image I remember most from that video was the joy on the faces of the Texan Christians as priest, nuns and lay folk literally danced a jig together to the rhythm of the goodness of God.

Read the whole passage and ask God where and what he is asking you to give today—time, money, love, encouragement?

CL

Life-giving dance

Holding fast to the head, from whom the whole body,
nourished and held together by its ligaments and sinews,
grows with a growth that is from God.

Have you ever been to one of those village dances which starts
with one couple? Each of them brings in a new partner at the
end of the first phase. Every time the music stops the number of
dancers doubles, until everyone swirls to the same rhythm.

This passage reminds me of that. 'Nourished' is our 'arranging
a dance for a village' word again but the image is biological. The
parts of our bodies interact like a complex dance: antibodies and
bacteria, genes and hormones, the circulation of blood, lymph,
food and waste products, bones working with muscles and nerve
impulses. Controlled, consciously or unconsciously, by the head
(the brain), they promote growth, health, movement, action and
renewal. We're often encouraged to think of our Christian lives
in terms of personal holiness, but Christ's body on earth is more
than the sum of the individuals within it, and the life of Christ,
the true Lord of the dance, flows to us corporately. He can speak
to us individually but more often will comfort, encourage,
exhort, even direct through his people with their human arms
and voices.

Sure, we can dance on our own, but it isn't much fun!
Together we can resemble Jesus more closely, and form a dance
spectacle which will be noticed because it draws people in. But
only if we 'hold fast to the head' and don't go off doing our own
thing, like cancerous cells. Private jigs trip up other dancers. It's
in dancing together that we demonstrate what it's all about. As
Jesus said, 'By this everyone will know that you are my disciples,
if you have love for one another.'

Help us together to join in the fun, complexity and breathless laughter
of the village dance that you arrange, caring for those who are already
involved—and drawing in others too.

CL

Supporting the dancers

For this very reason, you must make every effort to support your faith with goodness, and goodness with knowledge, and knowledge with self-control… endurance… godliness… mutual affection… love. For if these things are yours and are increasing among you, they keep you from being ineffective and unfruitful in the knowledge of our Lord Jesus Christ.

'Support', or in some versions 'add to', is our 'arranging a dance for a village' word here. At first sight it looks like we're responsible for the whole of this daunting task, but read the whole passage. 'His divine power has given us everything needed for life and godliness' together with 'his precious and very great promises'. Phew! It's like when Paul declares he toils and struggles 'with all the energy that [God] powerfully inspires within me'. It's amazing how unskilled, unfit people can keep complicated steps going at a well-arranged barn dance, given a ploughman's supper plus a good caller and fiddle player. We don't become more godly by sitting back. Our 'dancing' requires effort, attention, discipline even— but the power and energy, the life in it, comes from the Lord of the dance. God has given us everything we need to 'escape from the corruption that is in the world… and become participants of the divine nature' (2 Peter 1:4). Wow! So he really does expect us to become effective and fruitful.

Thank God the passage speaks of these qualities *increasing* in us. I for one have two left feet and wouldn't like to say how many times I've tripped up over most of the issues listed. I'm so glad he promises forgiveness, mercies that are 'new every morning'. I'm so glad that he lavishes us with so much love that we can give some of it away.

I know these things need to increase in me, Lord. When you put me in situations where I have to learn about them, help me not to grumble or go under but to draw on your divine power and promises.

CL

Progress in the dance

For this very reason, you must make every effort to support your faith with goodness, and goodness with knowledge, and knowledge with self-control... endurance... godliness... mutual affection... love.

Dancers move in stately progress up a line, linking arms with goodness, self-control and godliness in turn. This list of heroic qualities will convince many of us that we've failed to make the grade in the Christian life. Our faith's not strong, and as for endurance...

But hang on, near the list's pinnacle of achievement comes 'mutual affection' or, as some versions have it, 'brotherly kindness'. Doesn't that sound wimpish by comparison with the rest? All of us show kindness and affection from time to time. But isn't that what the passage is saying? Goodness, knowledge and all the rest are all very well in isolation but without love and kindness towards others, what is the point?

When I worked in a library, our first job in the morning was to tidy the books that we'd arranged in exact order the previous day. 'This place would run perfectly if it weren't for the readers!' we'd joke to each other as we fished *Vegetarian Cookery* from the biography section, or *Topsy and Tim* from among the weighty reference tomes. In the same way most of us might scrape by in the self-control and even godliness departments if it weren't for certain people who keep annoying us or upsetting our plans. But God isn't asking us to dance solos in perfect conditions. Plenty of people will rub us up the wrong way, but that's how we learn— not by 'spiritual discipline' alone but from the tangled mess when we get things wrong!

Help me to be disciplined enough to 'tidy up' each day, asking for your help to put things right, drawing on your promises and encouraged by understanding that what looks like a mess is your way of schooling us in the dance, of making us more like you.

CL

Heavenly dancing

For in this way, entry into the eternal kingdom of our Lord and Saviour Jesus Christ will be richly provided for you.

Yes, 'provided' in this verse is that same word, 'arranging a dance for a village'. It conjures up an image of all kinds of people dancing into heaven: the Russian men doing those squatting kicks, Caribbeans limboing low through the gate, the Irish with dead straight backs, moving long legs while keeping their arms still. Some groups will form a conga line; others, to the strains of Hava Nagila, will link arms and move from side to side, as well as forwards. Break dancers, disco dancers, they'll all be there—ballet, Elizabethan, ballroom and all. What a colourful affair, that dance at the wedding feast of the Lamb! No one will trip over anyone else, or suffer from corns or two left feet. It won't be too hot; there'll be plenty of space for all and no 'wallflowers'; no one will be prevented from dancing by pain or disabilities. I dare say even the bagpipe music which accompanies the Scottish dancers will sound lovely. Rich provision indeed!

Interestingly, this passage follows the two previous days' readings. Having listed the 'heroic qualities' of a Christian, this is Peter's way of saying that the effort is truly worth it. Verse 10 says, 'Therefore, brothers and sisters, be all the more eager to confirm your call and election, for if you do this, you will never stumble.' Goodness or even heroism won't earn our way to heaven, but on the other hand we wouldn't enjoy the wedding feast if we spent all our time on earth wanting to go our own way and refusing to join in the village dance.

Your provision is indeed rich, Lord, for your word says, 'Our steps are made firm by the Lord, when he delights in our way; though we stumble we shall not fall headlong, for the Lord holds us by the hand' (Psalm 37:23–24).

CL

Dance in a circle

If I had said, 'I will talk on in this way,' I would have been untrue to the circle of your children.

Moving on from *epichoregon*, the Hebrew word translated 'circle' here (or 'generation' in some versions) has its roots in a Hebrew word meaning to move in a circle, gyrate or remain. It paints an intriguing picture, one I find helpful. In a group of Christians at any one time some will feel full of the joys of spring while others will be struggling for various reasons. A year later the individuals who've endured tough times may have emerged as the new strong ones, while formerly bouncy types may be encountering doubts and difficulties. If the whole group supports one another —links arms in a circle, so to speak—then we can prevent one another from stumbling and all dance on! If we become bitter or judgmental, if we don't seek out God as verse 16 says and find his perspective on people and events, then we are in danger of swapping a God-ordained supportive circle for a vicious spiral.

It takes perhaps just a kind word or touch to include people in the circle. I still remember one phone call from years ago, when I'd moved to a new town after leaving university. Though in touch with a church there I'd yet to get to know them well. I felt so supported, so included and cared for when one of the leaders' wives phoned to ask how I'd got on in my first day at work. It was the same years later, when I was ill in bed once, and a woman from church phoned to say, 'I've just made a cottage pie for my family and one for yours as well. It'll keep in the fridge. Will you be able to answer the door if I pop in round about four?' We didn't strictly need it. My husband can cook and we'd food in the freezer, but that cottage pie did such *good*!

Read the whole of Psalm 73.

CL

The 'handshake' dance

You have turned my mourning into dancing; you have taken off my sackcloth and clothed me with joy, so that my soul may praise you and not be silent. O Lord my God, I will give thanks to you for ever.

If you read the whole psalm, you'll meet a man on a roller-coaster ride with God. I can identify with that, so am grateful for yesterday's supportive 'circle' effect which evens things out a bit.

Several passages speak of God turning mourning into dancing. I picture one of those dances where you shake alternate hands with people as you progress up a line. You have to let go of one to grasp hold of another, and that, in life, is not as easy as it sounds. Our family had wanted to move for years and we all loved the new house, but the day before we moved suddenly it struck our children that we'd have to leave the old one behind. Why couldn't we keep both, they demanded? On the eve of getting married, having a first baby or retiring, the advantages of single, childless or worker status can suddenly feel overwhelmingly attractive again, but we have to let go of the old to commit to the new. Life, like dance, never stays static.

This passage speaks of throwing yourself into the new state, body and soul. In almost every culture song and dance are used to express joy—and, less frequently, sadness and loss. We can express our mourning to God as well as the joy in our lives, though many of our church services give scant room for this. But, even if everything in our own lives has gone pear-shaped we can still give thanks to God for ever, because of who he is.

Read Habakkuk 3:17–19: 'Though the fig tree does not blossom, and no fruit is on the vines… yet I will rejoice in the Lord… he makes my feet like the feet of a deer, and makes me tread on the heights.'

                                                                    CL

With my body I thee worship

Then the prophet Miriam, Aaron's sister, took a tambourine in her hand; and all the women went out after her with tambourines and with dancing.

I have a confession to make: I am not a dancer. The women of Israel who escaped across the Red Sea weren't Royal Ballet trained either, but somehow I think they did better than I did when following in a line of dancers in Accra, the capital of Ghana. In the big, outdoor Easter church convention lines of either women or men (never both together) would dance around the huge central square as they worshipped God. I could have watched the colourful costumes and smiling faces endlessly, enjoying the rhythm, the economy and grace with which even the oldest and largest of them moved in the blazing sun.

On the final day the ladies who had been translating for my friend and myself prevailed on us to join in. The pallor of our skin made us the focus of about 17,000 African eyes and I became so self-conscious that I forgot how my legs and arms worked. When a man pointed a camcorder at me, even zooming in on my feet, I knew it wasn't just the heat making my face redden and run with sweat. Most cringe-making of all was my realization, when watching a copy of the video back in England, that the African ladies behind me had been trying to imitate my jerky hops. I only hope the trend didn't catch on!

It didn't matter that I danced in a different way from them—a rich diversity of culture is to be relished. It did matter that I was so obsessed with myself that I forgot all about letting go and worshipping God. After the miracle of escaping from slavery in Egypt I can't imagine those Jewish women having the same problem!

Help me to forget about myself as I worship you with all my heart, mind, soul, strength—and body!

CL

Dancing with confidence

Let them praise his name with dancing, making melody to him with tambourine and lyre. For the Lord takes pleasure in his people; he adorns the humble with victory.

Our rabbit, which had been bred by my daughter's friend, died last summer after five-and-a-half happy years with the Leonard family. Feeling utterly bereft and rabbitless, we scoured local pet shops before finding the sweetest soft-grey dwarf lop, just nine weeks old. He stood up remarkably well to travelling back in the car, safe inside the cage we'd improvised—an old freezer basket attached to a seed-tray floor. But when we put this down on the lounge floor and opened the lid, terrified, he refused to move.

We lifted him out in the end but he didn't seem to know how to walk. We'd never had this trouble with Bun No. 1, but he'd been handled and kept outdoors, not shut up in a pet-shop cage since birth. Still, before long Little Grey Rabbit began to take tentative steps, sniffing suspiciously as he progressed. Within a week he was learning to run. He tended to veer sideways but we encouraged him like mad. Finally he discovered the joy of springing high in the air from a standing start, then dashing three times round the room at top speed. How we enjoyed watching our timid bun gaining in confidence, learning new skills and becoming more and more lively.

Whether we're dancing in worship (a very scriptural thing to do) or learning to throw ourselves into other areas for which he's created us, or simply being ourselves, cradled in his hand and stroked by his love, how much more does the Lord take pleasure in his people? The human 'Little Grey Rabbits' of this world—the humble, the disadvantaged, the defenceless—are the very ones he chooses to adorn with victory!

Lord, when we feel timid, self-conscious or pathetic, help us to believe in you—because you believe in us!

CL

Dirty dancing?

As the ark of the Lord came into the city of David, Michal daughter of Saul looked out of the window, and saw King David leaping and dancing before the Lord; and she despised him in her heart.

Why? Surely Michal could see that David had reason enough to rejoice. After all, the ark, that visible sign of God's presence with Israel, was being returned to Jerusalem after a humiliating period when it had resided in the hands of their enemies, the Philistines. Could it have been that Michal considered that kings should behave in a more dignified fashion? I've heard it said that, in those days before boxer shorts or trousers were invented, a man who 'danced with all his might' could reveal rather more than he intended. But David always was a man who threw himself into things. Whether in battle, friendship with Jonathan, sin or repentance, he never did things by halves—which is interesting because he is described as a man after God's own heart.

Did Michal despise David because she didn't believe that much in God herself? Many of us have done the same thing— stuck the label 'fanatic' on anyone who is more definite or enthusiastic about their beliefs than we are ourselves. 'Look at her dancing, the show-off. Doesn't she look ridiculous?'

Of course people *do* sometimes use dance (or any Christian ministry) for wrong motives—to show off, even to attract sexual attention—but it's pretty clear that David's joy and thankfulness in the Lord were genuine. Singing and shouting weren't enough, he *had* to dance, just like the crippled beggar at the Gate Beautiful, who, after Peter had prayed for him, went 'walking and leaping and praising God' (Acts 3:8). Somehow I think that he and David were more godly than Michal—or all those lepers who never even thanked Jesus for their healing!

Father, help me to express my thankfulness to you with all of my heart —and to rejoice with those who rejoice in you, however exuberantly.

CL

Jesus at the disco?

' "We played the flute for you and you did not dance; we wailed, and you did not mourn." For John came neither eating nor drinking, and they say, "He has a demon"; the Son of Man came eating and drinking, and they say, "Look, a glutton and a drunkard, a friend of tax collectors and sinners!" Yet wisdom is vindicated by her deeds.'

Jesus knew how to celebrate and have a good time. It's likely, if he turned water into vast quantities of the finest wines at a Jewish wedding, that he danced as well. I steer well away from nightclubs and even in my youth hated noisy, smoky discos. But I bet Jesus would be there, with people who need him. After all he let a prostitute massage his feet with perfume and wipe them with her hair (yes, those are sexual practices!). Yet he stayed pure in thought and action as he gave her love, acceptance and a new start.

Jesus always surprises and sometimes affronts us. At least wild John the Baptist out in the desert, eating honey and locusts matched the image of a holy prophet, or an Essene, as he urged repentance and baptized people. Jesus, well he wasn't your normal rabbi, zealot or *anything*.

Jesus didn't do what anyone expected of him; he simply obeyed God. Sydney Carter's song has Jesus as 'Lord of the Dance' showing (rather than telling) us how to live. It's not by a series of laws or patterns. If we're to follow him, the dance will lead us on some surprising turns. Jesus never healed a person in the same way twice. He included many but drove others away. When people expected his stories to make things clear he told others so they wouldn't understand.

Help me not to make you in my own image—tame and predictable—not to water you down, but to expect surprises in the dance of life that you arrange.

CL

Dance of death... and life

For everything there is a season, and a time for every matter under heaven... a time to weep, and a time to laugh; a time to mourn, and a time to dance.

One trouble about these 'times' is that they don't always arrive at convenient or planned-for moments. Late one beautiful summer afternoon my father-in-law phoned in distress—his wife had been rushed by ambulance to a cancer hospital. I did *not* feel like going to set up and speak at a 'light-hearted literary evening' arranged by our local Churches Together in the library. But as it had been planned for months there was no escape until I returned home exhausted around eleven, far too late to phone for news. Several busy months and lots of worry later, she was pronounced clear of cancer and we could 'dance' again.

'I was commuting into London like a perfectly normal person, one minute,' a mature Christian woman told me, 'and an hour or so later was sitting on an Old Bailey jury, hearing all kinds of details I really didn't want to know about a series of sex offences, feeling indignant, as if it wasn't any of my business.'

The dance in which God leads us doesn't always take us where we want to go. In fact some of its twists and turns can leave us with a distinct sense of unreality. At such moments, when we don't know what to make of our conflicting emotions and desires it's comforting to know that 'our times are in his hands'. He never promised us an easy life, but he did promise to be 'God with us'—our comforter when we're mourning, our partner when we're dancing and a light for our path when we're confused and in the dark.

It's worth noting that the negatives described in Ecclesiastes 3 happen 'under heaven'. Praise God that *in* heaven there'll be no weeping, mourning, death, loss, hate or war.

Thank you that you're with us now and that you are taking us to glory!

CL

Having a ball

Now his elder son was in the field; and when he came and approached the house, he heard music and dancing. He called one of the slaves and asked what was going on. He replied, 'Your brother has come, and your father has killed the fatted calf, because he has got him back safe and sound.'

During the past year our house-group has prayed for three people who weren't right with God and who were dying before their fullness of years. It was great when they responded to his love, but when each died we had mixed feelings. Not only would certain of us miss these individuals, but they wouldn't be part of God's kingdom here on earth. Rereading this story has made me realize that God has a different perspective. He'll be throwing a party with music and dancing, because those who were lost are found.

The elder brother in Jesus' story of the lost son had more than mixed feelings. He plumped wholeheartedly for resentment—and for years I sympathized with him, secretly. How unfair that he'd worked hard and been obedient all these years and his rotten dad hadn't given him so much as a birthday present! But then I saw it. Of course Father God would have given plenty of presents and parties to his older son as well, because he's like that. However, some people are not very good at accepting presents, or at relaxing and having a ball. Toiling away in the fields and back rooms, the older son had refused to join in any of the dances - but now that the attention fell on his profligate but repentant brother his years of resentment boiled over. He wasn't lost because he had strayed outside of God's family but because he refused to count himself in or believe himself loved—because, in effect, he he'd misunderstood the Lord of the dance!

'Daughter, you are always with me, and all that is mine is yours! May I request the pleasure of your company now for this dance?'

CL

Security

Even the sparrow has found a home, and the swallow a nest for herself, where she may have her young—a place near your altar, O Lord Almighty, my King and my God.

Each April, I would marvel at this tiny bird. It had only a small beak, yet, with much skill, dexterity and perseverance, it had fashioned a nest out of twigs and dried leaves. It had positioned the nest so that, cradled in the fork of a branch and hidden by overarching leaves, there was a snug, secure shelter for her young.

Psalm 84:3 pictures the birds that have nested near the altar of God and illustrates the blessing of knowing God and coming freely into his presence. The sparrow is a common bird, but Jesus says that not even one of them is forgotten by God and that you are worth more than many sparrows (read Luke 12:6–7). The swallow, a migratory bird, has a homing instinct, and God has also placed a kind of homing instinct in us. Ecclesiastes 3:11 says, 'He has also set eternity in the hearts of men.' Indeed, God longs that our restless hearts may find our home in him. Even to those who have rejected him, Jesus says, 'How often I have longed to gather your children together, as a hen gathers her chicks under her wings'(Luke 13:34).

The nest pictures a place of rest, security and provision. There are other blessings of knowing God. The psalmist proclaims in verses 5–7 the blessing of finding strength in God. In the journey of life, we need this transforming strength. Without it, our sorrows can breed bitterness and cynicism. With it, the valley of sorrows can become a place of springs because of who God is. God is a sun and shield (v. 11).

Come and nestle close to him. Rest in him. Let the light of his life shine into all the shadows that threaten to overwhelm you. Let the Lord rule over the circumstances that are out of your reach. Let his Holy Spirit arise within you like a refreshing, flowing spring.

CT

Strength

And the God of all grace, who called you to his eternal glory in Christ, after you have suffered a little while, will himself restore you and make you strong, firm and steadfast.

Peter had experienced personal weakness and failure: he had denied Jesus three times. He thought he was strong enough to weather tough times, but self-confidence is very different from confidence in the Lord. In these verses, Peter shares with us how to find strength in the Lord.

The first step, in verse 6, is to humble ourselves under God's mighty hand. This involves facing up to the fact that we may not be able to help ourselves. With all honesty, we admit our inadequacy and ask God for help. This shifts our focus from ourselves to the Lord who is mighty.

A second step is in verse 7: to unload all our anxiety on the Lord. Worries and fears sap our strength and trap us in the false idea that no one can understand or even care about our situation. We need to unburden and freely talk to him about whatever weighs us down. The Lord is willing to carry us and our burdens. Read Psalm 68:19 and Isaiah 46:4.

In verses 8–9 is the third step: we choose to control our thoughts and feelings. Letting them run riot can cause us to stumble into the devil's trap. We can resist the devil by standing firm in the faith. By Jesus' death and resurrection, he has broken the power of the devil over our lives.

Finally, receive the promise in verse 10. The picture is that of a ship that has weathered a storm and is now repaired, refurbished and ready to be launched out. Peter experienced how Jesus lovingly restored him and strengthened him by pouring out the Holy Spirit.

I pray that out of his glorious riches he may strengthen you with power through his Spirit in your inner being (Ephesians 3:16).

CT

Comfort

Praise be to the God and Father of our Lord Jesus Christ, the Father of compassion and the God of all comfort.

Pain cries out for comfort. Whether it is a scratch on a toddler's knee or a threatening lump, the strain of a misunderstanding or the stress of being Christian in a hostile environment, we seek for comfort. But Paul tells us that God's comfort is not a mere pain-reliever or an escape valve but transforms us in our weakness.

The Lord is the God of all comfort. His comfort is sufficient and we need not look elsewhere to add on to it. His comfort actually means the Lord himself coming alongside. Jesus said that the Holy Spirit is the Comforter to be with us for ever (John 14:16). He comforts us in all our troubles. Whatever our personal pain, his comfort reaches us, touches us, and matches our distress. More than this, the comfort overflows. God gives comfort generously, abundantly, so that it can be shared with others. So, our own experience of trouble and comfort actually is a growth process. God is actually training us to comfort others.

God's comfort comes to us in many ways. We are comforted as we read an encouraging word from the Bible (Psalm 119:50; Romans 15:4). When Paul first visited Corinth and was met with hostility, the Lord appeared to him in a vision to comfort him (Acts 18:9–10). Jesus comforted the paralytic whose sins he forgave and the woman whom he healed (Matthew 9:2, 22).

We do not know exactly what trouble Paul was referring to, but it was unbearable; they were unable to help themselves. They had to rely on God and they were delivered from deadly danger. Paul also recognized that they were helped by the prayers of many. So, Paul now shares with us what he has learned: trust God and pray for each other.

Ask God to comfort someone in need and use you to offer comfort.
                                                                    CT

Forgiveness

'Then neither do I condemn you,' Jesus declared. 'Go now and leave your life of sin.'

'It is so hard to forgive.' 'Forgive? Perhaps. Forget? Never!' 'How can I ever forgive myself?' Underlying all these sentiments is our inability to forgive, which underlines our need for God's gift of forgiveness.

In our reading for today, a tense, dramatic incident unfolds. A private affair is dragged before public eyes. This woman was caught in the very act of adultery, but her accusers were more concerned with catching out Jesus than with morality, justice or mercy. Jesus' response to the accusers was, 'If any one of you is without sin, let him be the first to throw a stone at her.' Only Jesus, the sinless one, has the authority to judge. Not the woman. Not the accusers. Not any one of us. We may be like the woman struggling with secret sins, or like the accusers ready to judge and condemn others and unwilling to forgive. We are all sinners in need of God's forgiveness. Jesus did not condemn this woman but he did not ignore or condone her sin. He forgave her and told her to leave her life of sin. This is the heart of God and the power of his gift of forgiveness in transforming our lives.

The Lord is always willing to forgive (Psalm 86:5). When God forgives, he also forgets our sins. Read Psalm 103:12; 130:3–4. With his gift of forgiveness comes freedom from the power of sin and the haunting fear and taunting shame that often trap people in sin. With forgiveness, God also gives us his resources so that we can move on and start anew. Read 2 Corinthians 5:15–21.

If we confess our sins, he is faithful and just and will forgive us our sins and purify us from all unrighteousness (1 John 1:9).

CT

Peace

Peace I leave with you; my peace I give you. I do not give to you as the world gives. Do not let your hearts be troubled and do not be afraid.

What comes to your mind when you think of the word 'peace'? The elusive, fragile goal at a political negotiating table? The tantalizing, far-from-the-crowd hide-out? The breathing space of time all to yourself? These comforting words were spoken by Jesus to his beloved disciples when their world was about to fall apart.

The gift of peace is *his* peace, the peace that only Jesus can give and the peace that is evident throughout his earthly life. During those forty days of fasting in the desert, in physical weakness, Jesus could face the devil's temptations with calmness and clarity of mind. Constantly confronted by hostile authorities, Jesus continued to teach and minister without fear. It was as the prince of peace that he rode on a donkey to enter Jerusalem. In the face of an armed mob, false accusations and death, the innocent victim displayed a poise that demonstrated that he was very much in control. The peace that Jesus has comes from this: Jesus knew who he was and where he was in God's plans. Read John 13:1, 3.

This peace is found only in Jesus. 'In me you may have peace. In this world you will have trouble. But take heart! I have overcome the world' (John 16:33). So after his death and resurrection, when Jesus first appeared to his fearful disciples, his first words were, 'Peace be with you.' He gives us peace with God (Romans 5:1). He gives us peace that heals ethnic hostility (Ephesians 2:14–18). I saw this peace in my father's eyes as he faced death from cancer.

Read Philippians 4:5–9. What robs you of peace? Put into practice what these verses teach.

CT

John 15:1–11 (NIV)

Joy

I have told you this so that my joy may be in you and that your joy may be complete.

Over the doorway of a friend's house hangs a plaque in which are engraved these words: 'Joy is not the absence of sorrows. It's the presence of the Lord.' The joy that Jesus promises to us is not an emotional experience depending on the roller-coaster of circumstances. This joy has its source in the Lord and therefore is not earthbound, human joy.

Isaiah 62:5 depicts the Lord rejoicing over his people like a bridegroom rejoicing over his bride. Zephaniah 3:17 says that the Lord rejoices over his people with singing. In Luke 15, the parables of the lost sheep, the lost coin and the lost son emphasize the joy of the Lord over his lost children returning to him. The joy of the Lord is expressive, exuberant, festive, a celebration joy, comparable to when your favourite football team wins a game.

Jesus promises the fullness of his joy to his disciples, the fruit of remaining in Christ. This present period of sadness and suffering is limited and will turn to joy when we see him again (John 16:22). Joy is also a fruit of the Holy Spirit (Galatians 5:22). It is joy in the Lord himself. Therefore, the apostles experienced joy even in suffering persecution (Acts 5:41). Paul wrote a joyful letter to the Philippians while in prison awaiting possible martyrdom.

It is indeed outrageous joy, present in the midst of trials and troubles. Some years ago I had a memorable experience of this joy. I was in the labour ward where I was waiting for the birth of my baby but was traumatized to learn that her heartbeat had stopped. Whenever the overwhelming wave of sadness threatened to drown me, my conscious mind was like a cassette tape playing songs of praise and joyful hymns.

'Rejoice in the Lord always. I will say it again: Rejoice!' (Philippians 4:4). Take time today to find reasons to rejoice in the Lord. Focus on him and receive his joy.

CT

Wisdom

The fear of the Lord is the beginning of wisdom, and knowledge of the Holy One is understanding.

The world is getting wired up. People must become Net-wise. Information increases at an explosive speed. The rate of change with its repercussions on the way we live is frightening. We need wisdom to navigate a virtual world. So, do we resort to how-to books, management gurus and virtual learning institutes? Where do we get wisdom for changing times?

Knowing God is the starting-point of acquiring wisdom. The fear of the Lord is not the terror of the oppressed facing a despot but a healthy respect and reverence, a worshipful trust and obedience to the creator and holy God who loves us. Sometimes, our lives are ruled by other fears—of the future, failure, loneliness, lack. Yet the key to tackling all fears and uncertainties is a right relationship with the Lord (see Isaiah 33:6).

Wisdom is a gift from God (Proverbs 2:6). The Holy Spirit who is also called the Spirit of wisdom (Isaiah 11:2) and the Spirit of truth (John 14:16–17) is given to all God's children so that they can be wise. Thus, James encourages us that whenever we are in a sticky situation and do not know what to do, we should ask God for wisdom (James 1:5). Wisdom from God is not mere information but encompasses insights for decision-making, practical principles for living and spiritual understanding of God's ways and purposes.

James 3:13–18 also teaches us to discern between worldly wisdom and godly wisdom. Note that this kind of wisdom is revealed by the way a person acts and relates to others. We can use this passage to evaluate whether our lives reflect divine or worldly wisdom.

'By wisdom a house is built, and through understanding it is established; through knowledge its rooms are filled with rare and beautiful treasures' (Proverbs 24:3–4). How is the house of your life built? What treasures fill it?

CT

Backing a winner

*'Hosanna! Blessed is he who comes in the name of the Lord!
... Hosanna in the highest!'*

The street was noisy, messy with cloaks and palm branches, and
chaotic in its exuberant response to Jesus. This king came riding
on the colt of a donkey, symbolic of a king arriving in peace. The
people welcomed this king with the traditional greeting reserved
for pilgrims arriving in Jerusalem to celebrate the Passover:
'Blessed is he who comes in the name of the Lord.'

The air pulsated with hope mixed with pleas for help:
'hosanna, save us now!' But what did the people need saving
from—or what did they think they needed rescue from? Maybe
from oppressive tax burdens. From foreigners disrespectful of
their faith, traditions and worship. But did they have any idea
that they might need rescuing from themselves?

The people seemed convinced they were backing a winner, a
king who would rescue them and painlessly put right all that
oppressed them. They were filled with hope, optimistic that they
would be rescued from the mundane merry-go-round of everyday weariness. Or more seriously from cruelty and injustice.

How often I have pleaded for rescue ('Hosanna me, Jesus!')
and daydreamed that Jesus would dramatically take the hard bits
of life away—this cancer, my son's arthritis, my barrenness. That
he would whisk away the people that make my life so difficult—
those relationships that silence and shame me. I have often cried
out, 'A miracle, Jesus—just this one miracle.' Surprisingly, or
maybe not, that is not his style.

Rather, just as he did in Jerusalem so many years ago, Jesus
comes riding on a donkey, bringing peace into my life, not
magical escape—bringing himself into my life.

I find that profoundly comforting.

*Jesus, thank you for the comfort and quietness of your presence. In
that quiet comfort, hosanna us—save us. Save us from ourselves.*

EP

Scary student and business executive

'My house will be called a house of prayer for all nations.' But you have made it a den of robbers.

The following day, after entering Jerusalem in peace, Jesus unleashes his fury in the temple area. Fury at corrupt money-changers ripping off pilgrims of prayer. Fury at extortion by the high priest's henchmen selling sacrificial animals at inflated prices.

Tables flying, coins clinking, merchants scrambling, cattle and sheep stampeding out, doves flapping and squawking wildly in the confusion. Whip in hand, Jesus restores the temple as a house of prayer for all nations—a place of petition and praise.

Do you ever wonder what Jesus' face must have looked like in this passionate cleansing of his Father's house of prayer? Or what his voice sounded like rising above the pandemonium, shouting: 'My house will be called a house of prayer for all nations. But you have made it a den of robbers'?

It makes me wonder, what have we made God's house into in our own time?

Near the end of a conversation I had today with a very successful young business executive, he told me that he prayed every night before he went to bed. I nearly fell off my chair! He said he felt like his soul was crying out from inside of him, calling for help. Here is a young man, searching for God; and where are our houses of prayer for him—an unchurched seeker of God?

Two days ago I had a conversation with a young university student—body piercing extraordinaire—wearing a chain-link necklace with a heavy-duty lock. Pretty scary looking—and a student of genuine Christian faith. Not surprisingly, he was finding it difficult to find a church to fit into. Where is God's house of prayer for the young of our nation? For those of genuine faith seeking a place of prayer?

These conversations have made me stop and ask what Jesus would see if he walked into our churches today? A house of prayer or a den of robbers?

EP

Entrusted with the house of prayer

Be on guard! Be alert! ... You do not know when the owner of the house will come back... do not let him find you sleeping.

It was all carefully planned. Party time Saturday night. Clean up before Mum and Dad return. Simple... well, not exactly. Our daughters hadn't counted on the unexpected guests turning up—drunk and disorderly! They hadn't counted on the overall mess, or the broken table, or the ripped-out light fixture. They hadn't counted on not being able to control the circumstances.

When we walked into our house on return from a week's retreat, something felt wrong. We couldn't put our finger on it right away but we soon saw the remnants of the party from the night before. We had trusted our daughters—and entrusted them—with our home, theirs and ours. They were just not ready for our return and reunion.

On Sunday, we read how Jesus entered Jerusalem as a king of peace. On Monday, we read how this king of peace re-established a place of prayer for all nations in Jerusalem. Today we read serious warnings by Jesus, calling his followers to be on guard—to be alert!

Alert for what? Alert for King Jesus to return to earth, and to be ready to meet him at that time. Jesus said there would be difficult, even terrible times before his return: earthquakes and famines, wars and rumours of wars, persecution of believers, false teaching and false teachers. But even through these difficult times, we are to be on guard and not asleep. We are to be ready for our king's return.

And just how will we be ready? By making every day of our lives fit for our king's return. By keeping his house a house of prayer rather than a house out of control. By completing the work he gives us each day—the work of belief and of love, the work of building up the family of God and of prayer.

Our biggest danger is falling asleep on the job!

EP

The goodness of extravagance

While he was in Bethany… a woman came with an alabaster jar of very expensive perfume, made of pure nard. She broke the jar and poured the perfume on his head.

The scene: a comfortable home in the suburb of Bethany. The time: the week of preparation before the major religious and cultural celebration of the year. The players: Jesus, good friends of Jesus, disciples of Jesus.

The scene opens with the potent aroma of an expensive, exotic perfume filling the room. A woman has broken an alabaster jar of nard and poured it on the head of Jesus, the religious teacher who is reclining at the table. He simply receives this extravagant and unusual gift from the woman.

Some of the guests in the house are expressing indignation. 'What a waste! She just dumped a year's worth of wages on Jesus' head. And he does nothing! It could have been sold and the money given to the poor.'

Well, they've got a point, haven't they… or have they? *What is the point?* The point is that Jesus loves our spontaneous gifts of love and affection, just as he loves to give spontaneous gifts of love and affection. Jesus' defence of the woman's gift of anointing is swift and clear: 'Leave her alone. You'll always have the poor with you. She has done a beautiful thing to me. What she has done will always be told with the gospel.'

How extraordinary! For Jesus this is a beautiful thing and for those around it is a waste. Jesus so graciously receives this extravagant gift of love and generosity from the woman as a gift of preparation for his death—one of the last acts of kindness before his death. And in return, Jesus gives her a beautiful gift of affirmation and acknowledgment. I want to be like that!

Oh God, let my heart be free and spontaneous in extravagant and extraordinary acts of love and blessing. Guard me from 'righteous' indignation.

EP

The body is weak

*Then he returned to his disciples and found them sleeping…
'Could you not keep watch for one hour? Watch and pray so
that you will not fall into temptation. The spirit is willing, but
the body is weak.'*

At the beginning of Lent I decided that I wanted to use this time
to discipline myself and remove some of the interminable busyness of my life. I had heard a brilliant talk challenging us to pick
something up for Lent rather than the usual giving something up
for Lent.

Yes, I thought. That was a great idea. I thought that for each
day in Lent I would be quiet, read the Bible and pray for one hour.
Piece of cake, I thought. Well, I expect you know what happened.
Two days into Lent, the busyness of my life completely obliterated
any thoughts of an hour of quiet—let alone space.

It wasn't that I didn't want to be quiet and meditate each
day—I was willing. But somehow all my busyness and all the
distractions of my life choked my intentions. It makes me think
of so many diets and exercise disciplines I've tried! But that's
another story.

The disciples were willing—Jesus knew that. He also knew
that their bodies were weak. They were tired and weary.
Tragically, they simply didn't understand what this was all about
until it was too late to support and care for Jesus and themselves.
How often have I missed such opportunities?

Jesus asked his disciples three times to watch and pray with
him. Just the day before, Jesus had talked with them about the
importance of staying alert so they wouldn't be found sleeping.
And here they are in the garden snoring up a storm. They missed
being with Jesus in his moment of need.

That night, when Jesus was overwhelmed to the point of
death (v. 34), in deep anguish over his impending death, they
snored on.

Us too?

EP

Bridging the gap

'My God, my God, why have you forsaken me?' … With a loud cry, Jesus breathed his last.

Jesus dying on a cross. *Can this really be the Son of God—the king who will save us?* Soldiers gambling for Jesus' robe as he hung in pain. *Caught in the moment, they miss the love of God.* The morbid curiosity of a man who wanted to see if Elijah would rescue Jesus from the cross. *Would he have believed if Elijah had?* A tough, hardened Roman soldier who hears Jesus' cry and utters, 'Surely this man was the Son of God!' *Was that belief or just observation?* Two thieves dying similar deaths with Jesus: one cynical, one believing. *Where would they be tomorrow morning?*

Could it be that these facets of human nature were part of the completion of God's plan of rescue for men and women just like them? Could it be that God would die alone in the midst of callous human nature, their eyes glued to his hanging body, waiting to see if he would jump down from the cross? Could Jesus do no more than look helpless and weak in comparison to the hardness of humanity around him?

Alongside stood the ever faithful women, still caring for Jesus in his suffering and death—just by being there. *Would they still have faith tomorrow?* Disciples peered from a distance, trying to make sense of their beloved teacher, so helpless, jeered and spat upon. *Was his teaching powerless too?* Men once blind, now miraculously healed, watched him die a gruesome death. *Would their eyes hold on to the light?* Lepers once barred from public spectacles pushed their way in to behold their miracle worker run out of miracles for himself. *What miracle will keep them in the Kingdom now?*

Unable to bear more, Jesus finally cries out: 'My God, my God, why have you forsaken me?' (v. 34). Jesus takes upon himself all human sin. The earth trembles and convulses as the Son of God gasps in death.

'With a loud cry, Jesus breathed his last' (v. 37). It is finished. Jesus dies.

EP

Lovingly wrapped in secrecy

So Joseph bought some linen cloth, took down the body, wrapped it in the linen, and placed it in a tomb cut out of rock.

The Son of God was dead, his work finished and complete. It was about three o'clock in the afternoon and evening was rapidly approaching. The body of Jesus would be left hanging until after the sabbath if not taken down before sunset. Joseph acted quickly to get permission from Pilate to remove Jesus' body. Although surprised at the quickness of Jesus' death, Pilate gave permission.

Joseph is a curious character in the death of Jesus. He was a prominent member of the Council—or the Sanhedrin. He was very probably at the trial of Jesus the night before when Jesus was judged and condemned. And, according to John, he was a secret disciple of Jesus (19:38–42).

Joseph is accompanied by another curious character— Nicodemus. Nicodemus, who came to Jesus at night for a conversation (John 3). Nicodemus, who was confused about having to be born again. What a curious pair.

These two once-secret disciples take Jesus' body down from the cross and prepare it for the grave. They caringly wrap the body in strips of linen and a mixture of myrrh and aloes, then lay Jesus in a new tomb. All the while the women watch to see where the body will be laid.

Jesus started his earthly life wrapped lovingly in strips of cloth by his mother and being gently laid to rest in a manger. When he was a child, Magi from the east brought the baby Jesus gifts, including myrrh. Now, in his death, at the end of his earthly life, he is wrapped lovingly in strips of cloth and myrrh by two secret but faithful disciples and is gently laid to rest by two men who loved him, in a tomb carved in stone.

And when Jesus' body is laid to rest on that eve of Passover, Joseph of Arimathea, Nicodemus and the women return to their homes to rest on the sabbath.

EP

He is risen! He is not here

'Don't be alarmed... He has risen! He is not here. See the
place where they laid him...' Trembling and bewildered, the
women went out and fled from the tomb. They said nothing to
anyone, because they were afraid.

Finally the sabbath is over. Dawn is just beginning in the east.
And the women bustle about with their spices and supplies to
anoint and preserve Jesus' body. Wrapped in their own feelings
of grief, of disbelief, and of loss, these faithful women leave to
perform their last act of caring for Jesus.

And suddenly, an obvious question: the stone. Who will roll
the stone away from the entrance of the tomb? And yet they
keep on walking, wondering about the stone and how they will
move it. When they arrive, the stone has already been rolled
away. What a relief! They can complete the final preparations of
Jesus' body—a final act of love to bring closure to Jesus' death.
So they enter the tomb looking for Jesus' body. Instead they find
an angel, saying, 'Jesus has risen!'

They are alarmed and terrified. Even after the angel tries to
calm their alarm, they tremble in bewilderment. Risen? What on
earth does 'risen' mean? Has he been stolen? Is this a political
thing? Have we simply come too late? But 'risen'—what is that?
They leave the tomb and flee!

So would I! I've never met an angel or a resurrected person.
But I have often gone looking for Jesus only to discover he's not
where I expect him to be. And he doesn't look like I expect him
to look! Just like the women, I too am often bewildered, not
knowing where to find him or what to do with his angels.

Sometimes I arrive to discover that he's just left. Sometimes I
just don't get what's going on. I think the women just didn't
know what to make of this—they didn't know what was going
on.

So what was going on? Jesus is going on—he's alive!

Alleluia! He is risen. He is risen indeed.

EP

116

Rolling away the stone of grief

'Woman,' he said, 'why are you crying? Who is it you are looking for?'

The pain and the loss at his death were overwhelming. Jesus, this teacher, who knew her so well and still loved her, had given her dignity and respect. He had called seven demons out of her and still he let her journey with him and with his disciples. When others had discounted and disrespected her, Jesus honoured her.

In the imagination of memory, she can remember the look of love in his face, his tenderness with her brokenness, his gentleness.

Now he was dead.

All she wanted to do was to weep and mourn his death and say goodbye to him—but his body was gone. There would be no last farewell. Here in the garden, she felt as empty as the tomb. Her grief felt like a huge stone, sunk deep within her, lodged permanently in place within her.

And then she heard something. Her name—*her own name!* And that voice. She knew that voice. No, it couldn't be! Whirling around, not daring to believe, her tears gave way to sight and she saw him. He was alive! He was there in front of her. She flung her arms around him and cried out, '*Rabboni!*' (Teacher).

The stone was dislodged and rolled away. Her grief turned to joy and her mourning to amazement. Jesus immediately unwrapped her arms from around him and gave her a mission: 'Go and tell.' And that's exactly what she did. She went and found the disciples and told them what had happened: 'I have seen the Lord!'

We have so many stones lodged in place deep within us from losses and grief in our lives. And like Mary we continue to wait outside these tombs of life. Perhaps it's time to turn from these tombs and see Jesus.

Jesus, come and find us in the graveyards of our life and gently call us by name. Come and find us.

EP

Rolling away the stone of blindness

*Then their eyes were opened and they recognized him, and he
disappeared from their sight. They asked each other, 'Were not
our hearts burning within us while he talked with us on the
road and opened the scriptures to us?'*

Deep in conversation, trying to make sense of the events of the
last week, two disciples walk along a road together. Jesus surrepti-
tiously slides into place alongside them and, unrecognized, he
joins their discussion and their journey.

These disciples are amazed that this newcomer to their conversation seems ignorant of the facts of the last week. Didn't he
know about this Jesus? So they tell the story of Jesus. During the
conversation Jesus begins to challenge and push their thinking
while opening the scriptures where they were blind in their
understanding.

At the end of their journey they urge Jesus to stay the evening
with them. During dinner Jesus takes bread, breaks it and gives
thanks. Suddenly their blindness turns to understanding and
they *know*: it is Jesus. He *is* risen! He *is* present!

That's just the way it happens, isn't it? We get so busy trying
to figure things out and trying to make sense of things that we
are often blind to the fact that Jesus is right in the middle of our
figuring out. And then suddenly, like a match being struck in a
dark room, our hearts burn within us and we see. Only problem
is, Jesus seems to have gone on. And we find ourselves running
—somewhere, to someone—trying to find someone to share our
excitement with: 'It is true! The Lord is alive and is with us.'

How often we miss the smile of Jesus on the train, or a
kindness in the supermarket, a thoughtfulness in our office, or
someone asking us how we are. And we simply miss Jesus
because we are so wrapped up in our own thoughts.

*Jesus, roll the stone of our blindness away that we might see you in
new ways, in new places, in new people today.*

                                                                    EP

John 20:19–23 (NIV)

Rolling away the stone of fear

*On the evening of that first day of the week, when the disciples
were together, with the doors locked for fear of the Jews, Jesus
came and stood among them and said, 'Peace be with you!'*

They had talked with Mary, who had seen Jesus, and Peter and
John had run and discovered the empty tomb. So the disciples
called an executive meeting—to talk, strategize, and make sense
of what all this meant—in secret, behind locked doors. They
were frightened for their own lives, terrified that they too would
be killed because of their association with Jesus.

Suddenly, without warning, Jesus stands among the huddled
disciples and speaks, 'Peace be with you!' With those words
come memories of crashing waves calmed, of howling winds
silenced, of clutching hands cramped on the boat gunnels in a
storm, of fishermen fearing for their lives. Jesus' words from that
storm come back: 'Why are you so afraid? Do you still have no
faith?' (Mark 4:40).

Jesus understood their fear of death—he had just come from
there. So he speaks peace to them huddled in fear behind locked
doors, struggling with questions of faith. Then Jesus shows the
disciples his hands and side—eternal wounds that prove he
understands their fears.

Finally, they get it! It all begins to make sense.

But Jesus doesn't stop there. He gives them a mission: 'As the
Father has sent me, I am sending you. Be my hands, be my feet,
be my words, be my heart in the world as I was for our Father in
heaven.'

My heart misses a beat reading Jesus' mission for his disciples.
Doesn't Jesus get it? He has just been killed for being holy hands
and feet—and he has the scars to prove it! To be sent as he was
sent was a high-risk proposition. No wonder disciples need the
gift of peace! The stone of fear begins to move.

And then another gift: 'Receive the Holy Spirit.' They are
not alone. Nor will they ever be alone. The Spirit will always be
with them.

                                                              EP

Rolling away the stone of doubt

'Unless I see the nail marks in his hands and put my finger where the nails were, and put my hand into his side, I will not believe it.'

Where was Thomas the night before, when Jesus showed up in the disciples' meeting? Was he out walking alone on the hills? Struggling with the faith he had put in Jesus—his uncompromising honesty with himself about what he believed?

Perhaps Thomas' way of struggling through his grief and his confusion was by being alone. His world was suddenly more chaotic than it had ever been and that probably didn't sit easily on his shoulders. And so he missed the disciples' meeting and Jesus' blessing of peace. He also missed when Jesus showed the other disciples the wounds in his hands and his side.

When Thomas did finally meet with the disciples they must have bubbled out their encounter with Jesus. But Thomas cannot pretend to believe when he doesn't. How can he? It doesn't make any sense. He cannot find a parking space for resurrection in his head. He has to be sure on this one. And at this moment, he wasn't.

There are so many things that I wrestle with in my head that just don't seem to find a parking space there—like resurrection; or believing that God really will take care of me, I don't have to do it all by myself, or believing that God really does love me.

But later, at another meeting, still behind locked doors, Thomas is with the disciples. And Jesus shows up again: 'Come and see, Thomas. Stop doubting and believe.' Thomas' response is instantaneous and clear: 'My Lord and my God!'

Jesus rolled the stone of doubt away. Thomas is a believer.

Thank you, Jesus, for the respectful and loving ways in which you seek us out in our places of doubt. But some of our stones of doubt, Jesus, are very big and very stuck. Dislodge them. Roll them away. Release us into belief.

EP

Rolling away the stone of alienation

'Simon, son of John, do you truly love me more than these? ... Simon, son of John, do you truly love me? ... Simon, son of John, do you love me?'

Late one post-resurrection day, Peter heads off to go fishing—that was his job, after all—and some of the disciples decide to join him. After fishing all night without much success they head for shore. Someone on the shore calls out and suggests they cast the net on the right side of the boat. They do, and catch 153 fish! John realizes that the 'someone' on shore is Jesus and tells Peter. And in true, impulsive Peter-fashion, Peter takes the plunge and swims to shore. Meanwhile the other disciples bring Peter's boat in and soon enjoy a breakfast cooked by Jesus.

After breakfast Jesus asks Peter, 'Do you truly love me more than these?' Three times Jesus asks this question. Peter must have immediately remembered how he had betrayed Jesus and three times denied even knowing him. *Doesn't Jesus understand how painful this is to Peter? Doesn't he understand the pressure Peter is under?* Of course, Peter is hurt, but three times his response is a simple, 'Yes, Lord, you know that I love you.' And with that extraordinary encounter, the broken relationship between Jesus and Peter is healed.

I always want Jesus simply to throw his arms around Peter and say, 'There, there, Peter. It's OK.' But Jesus never goes for sticking plaster, he always goes for major surgery. He knew that Peter needed deep reconciliation after he had betrayed Jesus—a deep surgical procedure of character. This was the right time for that painful surgical cut of correction.

Have you ever experienced Jesus' surgical skill, those deep cuts for character correction? I have. And I'm grateful that Jesus would be bothered to care enough to thoughtfully and carefully make the necessary incisions.

After surgery came a mission: 'If you love me, then take care of my people—my lambs, my sheep. Feed them. Care for them as I myself would.' And with that, Jesus rolled away the stone of alienation.

EP

Rolling away the stone of comparison

When Peter saw [the disciple whom Jesus loved], he asked, 'Lord, what about him?' Jesus answered, 'If I want him to remain alive until I return, what is that to you? You must follow me.'

After Jesus and Peter are reconciled, Jesus talks with Peter about how Peter is going to die. 'When you were younger you dressed yourself and went where you wanted; but when you are old you will stretch out your hands, and someone else will dress you and lead you where you do not want to go.'

These comments by Jesus must have been quite overwhelming for Peter. He had cracked under the pressure of Jesus' trial and crucifixion and now he was being told that he would die a similar death—whew! My mind would race right back into fear and panic and paralysis just at the possibility of suffering such pain.

Peter's way of dealing with Jesus' comment is to compare himself with the disciple John. 'What about him? How is he going to die?' Jesus says, 'What is that to you, Peter? Your task is to follow me.'

I'm just like that at times when I am frightened and want someone else's options. I skip right over my fear and my terror and jump into attack: 'Why do I get all the grunge jobs? Why can't I have John's place?' How easy to think that God is taking more notice of others and even likes them better.

So Jesus refocuses Peter. He reminds Peter that people's journeys are tailor-made. Not comparable, not transferable. One journey; one person.

Gently Jesus invites: 'Peter, you must follow me'—not John! That is our task as well—to follow Jesus wherever he leads us; to keep our eyes on him and the journey that belongs uniquely to us, and not into the tombs and deadness of comparisons and competition.

Jesus, keep rolling away our stone of comparison so that we can follow you into our unique journey.

EP

Does God have a face?

My heart says of you, 'Seek his face!' Your face, Lord, I will seek. Do not hide your face from me.

At six every evening, a small face would appear at the window of the house opposite us, looking eagerly down the road towards the station. Then, suddenly, it would vanish and from the front door a three-year-old body would hurl itself on to the pavement. Weaving between the streams of tired commuters, she made towards a tall man with a huge ginger beard, shouting, 'Daddy, my daddy!' When he saw her, he would crouch down and open his arms wide. I loved the way she would look up earnestly into his face as she told her news. 'I found a caterpillar, I put it in a matchbox for you, and I made some sticky cakes for your tea.' All the time she talked, her little fingers would stroke the ginger shredded wheat of his beard.

The God that the Bible portrays is not merely a creative force or a vague power of good, but a *person* who feels, thinks, communicates and wants to be known and loved in return. His face is mentioned many times, and so are his features: 'for the mouth of the Lord... has spoken' (Micah 4:4, NRSV); 'the eyes of the Lord range throughout the earth, to strengthen those whose hearts are fully committed to him' (2 Chronicles 16:9); 'my cry came before him, into his ears' (Psalm 18:6); 'smoke rose from his nostrils; consuming fire came from his mouth' (2 Samuel 22:9).

People would 'seek the Lord's face' when they wanted to come close to him. Another frequently occurring phrase, 'enquire of God', could be translated from the Hebrew as 'stroke the Lord's beard'. God longs for us to be that close to him. He longs for the kind of intimacy that delighted my neighbour when his daughter gazed up into his face and chatted to him as she stroked his beard.

Lord, I can't see your face, but show me how to look into it by faith. Amen.

JRL

What makes God smile?

The Lord bless you and keep you; the Lord make his face shine upon you and be gracious to you; the Lord turn his face towards you and give you peace.

On holiday last summer, it rained most days. As I sheltered in a seaside café one morning, I noticed a family at the next table. Comical but moving—that's how I would describe the doting smile on the father's face. The toddler was obviously his first child—the longed-for son of his dreams. The father's beaming smile followed him everywhere as he dashed between the tables on unsteady legs. Even when he covered himself from head to toe with ice-cream the father still smiled proudly, as he murmured, 'Just look at him feeding himself!'

People in the Bible often prayed that God's face would shine (smile) on them or be turned towards them: perhaps they wanted God to look at them as a new and besotted father looks at his first-born! And of course that is how God looks at us. He says we are the apple of his eye, his delight. His beaming smile follows us, too, all through the day, wherever we go.

Yet the Bible also tells us that God turns his face away from people who deliberately disobey him (Deuteronomy 31:17). He never abandons his children but we can lose his smile—that sense of being close and comfortable with him. One of my children behaved extremely badly once, when grandma came to tea. Later he came up to me and whispered, 'Mummy, I'm sorry, please make your face smile at me again!'

I used to think I had to wait until I went to bed at night before going through a long list of all the things I'd done wrong that day. I've since learnt not to wait that long. The moment I feel I've upset God I ask his forgiveness—then and there. It comes instantly, so long as we ask.

Lord, I want to live constantly in the light of your smile. Thank you for forgiving me so often and so quickly! Amen.

Read Psalm 31:14–20.

JRL

Another way of praying

As for me, I shall behold your face in righteousness; when I awake I shall be satisfied, beholding your likeness.

My friend Dave was born blind. When people urged him to pray for healing he used to smile and say, 'If the first thing I ever see is the face of Jesus, it will be worth waiting a lifetime for a thrill like that!' Dave died recently and I often imagine him sitting there gazing! The face of God may be invisible to us on earth, but we can still gaze—by faith.

On his way to work in the fields, an old French peasant used to slip into church and sit for a while, smiling up at the rafters. He did the same on his way home in the evening. Curious, the priest asked him what he was doing.

'I just look at him and he looks at me,' was the simple reply.

Once I used to feel guilty if my mind wandered while I prayed. Now I realize praying can also mean just sitting in God's presence, basking in his love.

The more you care about a person, the less important words are as a form of communication. I adored my father and spent every available moment with him, yet we could go for long walks together or sit by the fire for a whole evening without talking. We used to say we could read each other's thoughts just by the expressions on our faces, but to get that close to someone you do have to spend a lot of time with them.

We all need to make a point of coming face to face with God every day, to open ourselves to him, and to give him the chance to open himself to us. Not just for our benefit either—he actually enjoys looking at us. He says to each of us:

'Come then, my love; my darling, come with me. You are like a dove that hides in the crevice of a rock. Let me see your lovely face and hear your enchanting voice' (Song of Songs 2:13b–14, GNB)

JRL

I can't see his face!

And the Lord said, 'I will cause all my goodness to pass in front of you, and I will proclaim my name, the Lord, in your presence... But,' he said, 'you cannot see my face...'

Moses was said to talk to God 'face to face as a man talks to his friend'. Yet, today's passage shows that he only saw God's face by faith and not in reality. Elijah, another Old Testament 'friend of God', trudged forty days through the desert to encounter God. Yet, when he finally stood before him on Sinai, listening to his whispery voice, he hid his face in his cloak (1 Kings 19:12–13).

In Old Testament days God seemed so distant and powerful that people dared not even speak his name. Jesus came to show us what God is really like, saying, 'Anyone who has seen me has seen the Father' (John 14:9).

The only way to know God is to look at Jesus, and Moses and Elijah were finally allowed to do that. Once, when Jesus was standing on a mountaintop, he suddenly began to shine like the sun and the terrified disciples saw Moses and Elijah talking with him face to face (Matthew 17:1–8).

When one of my six children refused to look at me when I spoke to him it was either because he knew he had done something which would make me cross or I had done something to make *him* cross—such as refusing him sweets! When we don't feel like looking into God's face it may be for the same two reasons. Perhaps we don't want to let go of something we know is upsetting him: an unhealthy relationship, activity or self-indulgence might have become so important to us that it blocks out his face whenever we try to focus on it.

We can also be 'upset' with him over something he has allowed to happen to us or refused to let us have. When we are arguing with God our resentment hangs like a cloud between his face and ours.

Lord, may nothing come between your face and mine today.

JRL

John 1:41–42 (NIV)

When Jesus looks at me

*The first thing Andrew did was to find his brother Simon
and… brought him to Jesus. Jesus looked at him and said,
'You are Simon son of John. You will be called Cephas'
(which, when translated, is Peter).*

I wonder how Peter felt when he first looked into the face of
Jesus. The big, loud-mouthed fisherman was named Simon
('reed') because he was as easily blown about as reeds in the
wind. He was so weak, he changed his priorities according to the
people he was with; yet, as he stared at Jesus, he knew those eyes
were looking right through him, seeing not the man that he was
but the man he could become.

'You may be named after a wobbly reed, but you will be
known as Peter (the rock),' Jesus told him.

When we look into the face of Jesus we can't hide anything
from him. That can feel unnerving, but also comforting. Most
people judge us by our outward appearance, our achievements or
our past record. When Jesus looks at us he sees the person he
could make us into one day. He also sees all our struggles and
fears. The rich young man whose story is told in Mark 10:17–23
longed to follow Jesus but he was afraid. His money made him
feel safe, comfortable and a 'somebody' in this world. Jesus
looked into his face, challenging him with, 'Will you trust me to
provide everything you need, instead of relying on your money
to do that for you?' Mark describes the expression on Jesus' face
as he waited for the answer—'a look of deep love and longing'
(v. 21, Amp).

*Lord, I know that you look at me sadly, too, when I struggle with the
issue of where I place my dependency. I want to trust you for everything in life, but I find myself leaning on other things and other people
instead. I know you can see what I could become if only I were willing to let you change me. Thank you, Lord, for your uncondemning
love that accepts me as I am and loves me—whatever!*

JRL

The hidden face

They came to Bethsaida, and some people brought a blind man and begged Jesus to touch him. He took the blind man by the hand and led him outside the village.

When Jesus had just changed someone's life, he often said, 'Your faith has healed you.' I guess faith was easier when you could look up into that face and see the strength and compassion in the eyes of Jesus. The man in today's passage didn't have that advantage. As he stood in the crowded marketplace, feeling the crowds jostling around him, all he could do was grope out towards a voice in the darkness. Suddenly, he felt his hand grasped and held tightly by the work-roughened hand of a carpenter. Was he puzzled when he wasn't healed on the spot? Everyone was expecting that to happen. Murmurs of disappointment, even anger, must have followed the blind man as he stumbled away over the cobbles beside a complete stranger.

We don't know how far they walked, how long they spent together or what they talked about, but they would have been friends and not strangers when, at last, Jesus stopped in the peace and privacy of the countryside. Even then the miracle wasn't instant but gradual! Why did Jesus take so long? Making friends with that man mattered more to Jesus than just healing him because, to Jesus, our relationship with him is of paramount importance.

Isn't it frustrating when you pray for something but nothing happens? Like this blind man, we grope towards God by faith, feeling sure he must want to help, but then the waiting begins! Sometimes he really does seem to 'hide his face' (see Psalm 102:2), yet something vital is happening in that gap between the point where we begin to ask and the moment when our prayers are answered. He is teaching us to know and trust him. He wants us to walk by faith and not by sight (2 Corinthians 5:7).

Thomas said to him, 'My Lord and my God!' Then Jesus told him, 'Because you have seen me, you have believed; blessed are those who have not seen and yet have believed' (John 20:28–29).

JRL

The laughing face of Jesus

'If you obey my commands, you will remain in my love, just as I have obeyed my Father's commands and remain in his love. I have told you this so that my joy may be in you and that your joy may be complete.'

One summer we went to Europe for our holiday. The weather was awful! Mountain-walking was impossibly dangerous and poking round the shops was too tempting. The only places where we could keep dry, warm and financially solvent were the numerous, ornate churches. By the end of a fortnight I realized I had looked into the face of Jesus thousands of times, through icons, portraits, stained-glass windows or sculptures; but never once had he smiled back at me. The artists had all depicted him looking depressed, severe, disapproving, anorexic or downright cross!

I know Jesus was called the 'man of sorrows' and that he died in agony, but I am convinced he was also full of joy and laughed a lot. Some of the stories he told would have tickled the Jewish sense of humour of his time and had people rolling on the ground! Humans are attracted to joy but we avoid people who look stern or miserable; those crowds would never have flocked after Jesus if he had looked like all those portraits. The Pharisees would have approved of him, and he might have attracted the academics of his day, but it was the ordinary working people, like Peter, whose hearts Jesus won—and the poor, the disreputable, the drop-outs and no-hopers. One look at his face would have made them feel accepted and included, not frowned on and despised.

Joy is as catching as flu! My friend Liz is always laughing; she sees the funny side of everything, and after spending time with her I always feel better. As we look into the laughing face of Jesus we, too, can catch his joy and then pass it on to a sad world that needs his kind of refreshing joy so badly.

Lord, help me to see what you are really like and then to introduce the real you to others.

JRL

The disfigured face of Jesus

Then they spat in his face and struck him with their fists.
Others slapped him and said, 'Prophesy to us, Christ. Who hit
you?' ...
   They went up to him again and again, saying, 'Hail, king
of the Jews!' And they struck him in the face.

One Sunday, our six children got the giggles in church. It was
the sight of the visiting preacher that started them off, and he
was certainly the ugliest man I had ever seen. His face was
grotesquely disfigured, but the moment he began to speak the
children were riveted—tears replaced the laughter. Hesbon had
been a pastor in Kenya when terrorists attacked his village,
burning his house and church and murdering his family before
his eyes. Finally they battered his face to a pulp with the butt of
their rifles, yet, as he told us how Jesus had given him what he
called 'peacejoy' in the centre of his anguish, his mutilated face
shone with unearthly radiance.

   The face of Jesus does not only have laughter lines but it also
bears many ugly scars. Isaiah 52:14 (GNB) says: 'He was so disfigured that he hardly looked human.' His face will also be deeply
lined by other kinds of suffering. He knows what it feels like to be
rejected by the people you love, misunderstood by your family,
betrayed, abandoned, blamed unfairly, misunderstood and
excluded. He was single, lonely, poor, overworked, physically and
verbally abused, taken for granted, publicly disgraced, beaten and
apparently defeated. He understands, from personal experience,
almost anything we go through—except, of course, the searing
pain of guilt. Yet it was to spare us that—worst of all the emotions
—that he died in our place on the cross.

'Surely he hath borne our griefs, and carried our sorrows' (Isaiah
53:4, AV). Thank you that, at your cross, I can exchange my pain
for your 'peacejoy'.

Read Isaiah 53:1–11.

JRL

Reflecting his face

When Moses came down from Mount Sinai… he was not aware that his face was radiant because he had spoken with the Lord…

And we, who with unveiled faces all reflect the Lord's glory, are being transformed into his likeness with ever-increasing glory, which comes from the Lord.

The other day I met a friend who had just returned from a silent retreat at a convent. Her face literally shone. 'Perhaps it's fresh air and monastic soap,' I thought, but as she talked about all that the Lord had done for her I realized that her radiance came from inside. Like Moses, she had spent time alone with God—and it showed!

The small boy who played Gabriel in a nativity play I attended last Christmas froze completely at the sight of the audience. His first line was, 'Fear not!' but he was too scared to say it! The entire cast prompted him but still he stood, green with terror. Then suddenly he caught sight of his dad, smiling encouragement at him from the front row. He caught that smile, as if it had been thrown like a ball, and soon he was beaming round at us all, sharing his father's smile with everyone!

Sometimes we get very worried about what we are supposed to do for God, but I am sure he just wants us to be radiators! The one in my sitting-room stores electricity at night, while it's cheap, so in the morning it warms everyone who comes near it. If, however, I've forgotten to switch it on the night before, it remains icy cold. It is by spending time with God that we absorb and store the warmth of his love so that we can radiate it to everyone we meet.

Lord, today help me to remember to keep looking up into your face, over the heads of all those who will surround me. I know you love them, even the irritating ones. Let me catch your smile—and your attitude towards them.

JRL

DAY BY DAY WITH GOD

MAGAZINE SECTION

World on our doorstep

Fiona Barnard

I will never forget a conversation I once had with a Muslim friend about a famous Arabic poet called Shukri, who studied in Sheffield several decades ago. It was a chance remark she happened to make which has had a profound effect on me ever since. She mentioned that in the three years he lived here, he never entered a British home; any time away from study he spent wandering around the city's parks. I can still recall the sense of sadness and shame which I felt: this man came to our country and found no welcome. How awful, not only for him but also for those who might have been enriched by his friendship. I am certainly grateful for the way my Muslim friend, and now her family, have enriched my life.

The world has shrunk. I've heard it said in jest that our national dish is Chinese take-away. Indeed, that along with Indian, Italian, Mexican and Thai food is as popular as any traditional fish and chip fare. Even in everyday shopping, the produce may be labelled in English with household brand names, but there is every likelihood that the ingredients themselves were imported from other countries. What are the chances that the toys we buy will be 'made in China', or that the electrical goods we see will be Japanese or Taiwanese or Korean? Usually pretty high.

Multi-national

Indeed, it is not only multi-national products, but also people who are very much part of life in the UK. Men and women come for business, to study or do research, to escape repressive regimes, or to join their families. Some stay permanently, while others are only here temporarily. A number are actively sought and invited to help us: many of the best footballers playing for British teams are from Brazil or Italy or Holland.

I live in a small town on the east coast of Scotland, and am amazed at the way people find their way here from all over the world—*au pairs* from Eastern and Western Europe, refugees from Serbia, poets and philosophers from China and Turkey, scientists from Pakistan, Russia and India, medical researchers and administrators from Sudan and Egypt, students from Poland, Latvia and Libya, chefs from Italy and Hong Kong, business people from Japan, women from Thailand and Ukraine who have married Scottish men. The list goes on.

Why then do we imagine that missionary work is only when people (who are undoubtedly 'more spiritual' than ourselves) travel abroad to preach the gospel? Yes, Jesus did tell his disciples to go into all the world—yet at the same time, and uniquely in our own age, the world has come to us, to our doorstep. Many folk come from places where it is very hard for missionaries to obtain entry visas, and where the national church is weak and struggling. It could very well be that God has brought them to your neighbourhood, your college, your workplace—'to a place near you'—open to new ideas and friendships while away from family and political pressure, so that they might have the freedom and the opportunity to hear the gospel. They may even return as native missionaries to their own people.

Welcome strangers

'Strangers' are never far from the heart of God. Even amid all the important first instructions given to Israel, they were on his list of priorities for special care: 'Love them as you love yourself' (Leviticus 19:34). Looking forward to the end of history, Jesus declares that those who welcome strangers have welcomed him and will be rewarded with hospitality in his kingdom (Matthew 25:34).

Anyone who has travelled any distance knows that it is hard to be away from home, from family and friends, from the security of familiar surroundings and culture and language. I think of a very distraught phone call from a devoted Japanese mother. Naoko was almost in tears as she told me that the nursery where she had registered her little girl claimed to have no record of her. Wanting to make sure her daughter attended the best school, she insisted that she had spoken to a teacher and filled in a form months earlier. Had she misunderstood what they had told her? The class could not have been full at that stage. So—did they not like foreigners? She didn't know about other nursery schools in the area and did not have the confidence to speak on the phone with someone who might have a strong Scottish accent. Even if she did, would they make the same excuse? With no one else to talk to other than her husband, who was preoccupied with work deadlines, it seemed as though her world was falling apart and her precious daughter would never get an education.

Manfredi came from Milan to make pizzas in an Italian restaurant. He was ill for a couple of weeks and when he returned to work, he was told that he had no job. He didn't seem to have been in the place long enough to have any rights so resorted to the social security office. He desperately needed money, but was completely bamboozled by the pages and pages of questions which would intimidate even a native English speaker.

Narges, from an Arabic-speaking country, accompanied her father when he came to do some research at the university. The oldest of five children, she went to school for a while, but never mastered English properly. In response to the permissive society all around them, her father became increasingly protective of his teenage daughter, so that she was not even allowed to answer the phone in case it was a man on the other end. The few outings she was able to make were to the shops and to an English class, but also to the home of a volunteer language tutor who happened to be a

Christian and who was able to give her an Arabic New Testament when she returned to her own country.

Opportunities

For those who have eyes to see and a heart of compassion, there are real opportunities to reach out in friendship to the international community in our country. It may simply begin with a friendly exchange with the Bangladeshi shopkeeper or the lady at the Chinese take-away; it may involve inviting a mother at the school gate back with her child to play with your children, or having a business colleague and family over for a meal; it may mean offering your car to take a handful of overseas students to see local sights, or opening up your home for a student who has nowhere to go at Christmas time; it may lead you to helping as a language volunteer in the council-run 'English for Speakers of Other Languages', or to thinking how, as a church, you might go out in love and solidarity to those who often experience loneliness and discrimination and racism.

The other day I received an e-mail from someone who had only been in this country for three months, and who had come around to the house perhaps two or three times for a meal. 'You are my friend for life,' he said. I was so touched, not only that my awful cooking had not proved fatal, but because such a little could mean so much. My prayer, once again with yet another transient relationship, is that God would set in place the next link in the chain that will lead this person to Christ.

Fiona Barnard lives in Scotland. Her principal work is among international students, encouraging local churches to reach out in friendship to those temporarily far from home.

Intimacy

Christine Leonard

John came home from work smiling. 'Bob asked where we got you from,' he said.

Ever since university, John has worked for the same team of computer software engineers, and a month or so previously I'd joined them, for two mornings a week, as their secretary. Bob (his name, when spoken in his amazing Alabama drawl, lasted a good ten seconds) had arrived a month or so before me, on secondment from one of the company's software teams in the USA.

John realized that, while the rest of the engineers had met me at various social events, Bob knew me only as Chris, the new secretary. When John explained that I was his wife, Bob's face cleared. 'Oh, right! I thought you two were giving each other funny looks.'

It was a shame, really, because we could have strung Bob along for ages. He'd obviously sensed some kind of intimacy between us—and no, we hadn't been indulging in passionate embraces all over the open-plan office, not so much as a peck on the cheek, so far as I could recall. We've been married for twenty years, for goodness' sake, and we'd gone to work… well, to work!

Vibes

Nevertheless, Bob had picked up some vibes and I must say John and I felt pleased, as well as amused, to have been caught out having an 'affair' with each other! We wondered at first whether Bob had heard something unsubtle, like the time when I'd asked John, 'Could you pick up a frozen chicken from Sainsbury's for the weekend, love?' But we think he was working at the other end of the office at the time. He might have been around on one of the occasions when John, seeing me working later than expected, paused at my desk before going out for his lunch. 'Sandwiches?' he'd ask. It happened quite often.

'Yes, please,' I'd say, glancing up from my computer screen. Ten minutes later, I'd be unwrapping the pack he'd brought me. No money changed hands!

There again, why was it, when some machine failed to work, that this new secretary always ran for help to the same engineer? John would be leaning over her desk, his body close to hers, and perhaps there'd be an exchange of 'funny looks' and a muttered, 'Thanks, love!' She seemed… more respectful towards the others. She didn't treat them in the same way, and, in turn, none of them ever bought her sandwiches!

In such mundane ways my intimacy with my husband became obvious to a virtual stranger. It made me wonder whether the same is true of my relationship with Jesus. I've heard many talks in recent years about growing in intimacy with him, about how passion for him should fire my soul, my life. During the same period, on occasions I've felt his love far more deeply than ever before, but have found myself wondering about my passion for him in everyday life. Is my true love for him reserved for extraordinary moments, alone or in church, when the warmth of his passion sweeps me off my feet? If so, am I letting him down the rest of the time? For most of my hours I forget about him, or, at best, take him for granted. How terrible to say that I could be indifferent for even one moment to the love of the one who created the universe! On the other hand, whenever I build a wall which blocks God out with bricks of indifference or anger, hurt or plain selfishness, sooner or later I do miss him dreadfully and come running back, because his love is the most important thing in the world to me.

Communication

Bob's mistake made me think. I realized that I don't sit around going gooey-eyed about my husband all day. There are too many things to be done which occupy all of my thinking power. When John comes home in the evening it's rare for either of us to have much time to sit and chat, yet, after twenty years of sharing our lives, even brief conversations communicate far more than it might appear. I know, too, that if I really need to talk at length about something, he will stop and listen. When he has to work abroad for a few days I feel empty and miss him terribly. I miss knowing that he'll be there to sort things out should the washing machine flood or the car refuse to start; I miss his warmth in the bed at night and most of all I miss him as a friend.

So many little things are bound up in a relationship of trust and love. If John sees me working through lunch-time, he cares enough to realize that I'll be hungry and so buys me sandwiches. This doesn't need long discussion, though it helps if I express appreciation from time to time. And we may not be thinking about each other every minute but our relationship affects our behaviour. I'm not going to flirt with the other guys in the office when John's away, just as he's never become intimate with any other secretary (even if he has a special licence for that kind of thing with me!).

In everyday life my conversation with Jesus is on the level of, 'Sandwiches?' 'Yes please!' But that kind of thing pre-supposes a deeper relationship, with a history. Strangers don't act like that towards one another. Sometimes, when I really need help, he does come close, not touching my body with his as he leans across the desk to sort out some broken machine, but reaching deep into my life to touch some attitude which needs attention—ouch! Usually the 'funny look' which follows reminds me of Christopher Robin hugging Winnie the Pooh close, and whispering, 'Silly old bear!' His love is unconditional and it melts me.

Behaviour

And our relationship informs how I behave. Oh, I get things wrong. I do things which I shouldn't and fail to do numerous things which I should, but whatever the prayer book says, there *is* health in me. To deny that is to deny that Jesus makes any difference to me at all. It's so easy to focus on the negative—I should love him more, pray more, pour myself out continually for others, be more holy. But without him I'd be horrible and in a mess! With him... well, his love can't fail to inspire *some* compassion, *some* goodness from time to time in a person, can it? Even if that person is me... or you!

If my love for John is evident, even when I'm not thinking about it, it's because that love is real, it's rooted deep. It's not only lasted but has become more secure despite irritations, misunderstandings, rows, hurts, mistakes, sickness, screaming babies, sleepless nights and the traumas of sharing our lives with two teenagers of our own making. I could say the same about my love for Jesus. Of course I pray that it grows. I pray that I will become more like him and that my love for him will shine out more and more. But thinking about Bob's mistake and writing this has encouraged me. I *do* love both John and Jesus and they love me, in a way that's real not only when I'm floating on the passion of cloud nine but in the ordinary details, the intimacies of everyday life. My love's so far from perfect, but love grows in an atmosphere of acceptance and thankfulness, and shrinks if we worry and fret about it. Intimacy with Father, Son and Holy Spirit sounds either scary or far too good to be true, but thank you, God, that even ratbags like me can enjoy it, right now!

Chris Leonard is a regular contributor to *Day by Day with God* and is the author of *Affirming Love*, published by BRF. You can find further details on page 155, and an order form on page 157.

Perfectionists?

Ruth Leak

Aunt Hannah lives in a bungalow on the outskirts of a busy town. Now she is retired, there is nothing she enjoys more than watching the birds from her conservatory. She has a man to help with the garden and he is very thorough—too thorough for Hannah.

'If only he was not so meticulous,' she says, 'he would be able to do much more.'

It reminds me of a discussion I heard on the radio. Perfectionists, it was claimed, are not the people to get things done. Far better to get someone who completes a task even if there are bits that could have been done better.

Pressures...

Not everyone subscribes to this point of view and at times we feel tremendous pressures on us to be perfect. We are tempted by the concept of the 'ideal home' and watch endless TV programmes featuring home and garden makeovers. And what about the perfect hourglass figure? How many of us have spent hours standing sideways in front of the mirror, breathing in and tucking away the bits of us that we prefer not to be seen?

Sadly, not all the illustrations are amusing. Janet is a young mum trying to juggle work, a young family and running the home. The cracks are beginning to show and she knows it. 'The problem with me,' she says, 'is that "fine" is not good enough. I want perfect.'

The same conflict is reflected in our spiritual lives. Constantly aware of the eyes of the outside world, we want our churches to be fashionable, 'cool' places to be and our church leaders to be 'together' people with plenty of street cred. We want the people who go to church to be well-balanced and respectable—heroes, almost, or maybe perfect Christians.

Perfect Christians? Is it possible? We sometimes act as though it is and actually pursue the notion to surprising extremes, getting ourselves into all sorts of emotional knots on the way. We are particularly good at this when it comes to illness. 'Why am I feeling ill?' we ask. 'Is it because God is trying to tell me there is something wrong with my life?' It's true that it can be a good thing to review our lifestyles and learn lessons from that, but all too often we can be over-anxious in our approach and wade into a period of unhealthy introspection. Our Bible study and prayer times become overshadowed by the thought that *today* is the day God will reveal the problem. Ironically, anything else he may want to reveal to us is crowded out by our anxiety.

The same thing can happen in all sorts of circumstances.

'Why can't I find a job?'

'Why isn't God giving me the spiritual gift that I desire so much?'

Questions like this can actually make us feel worse. As well as coping with the original problem, we have the added burden of guilt.

Perfection?

In Matthew 5:48 we read Jesus saying, 'Be perfect, therefore, as your heavenly Father is perfect' (NIV). Surely he would not have asked us to aim for something that is unachievable? It is easy then to take one further step (not mentioned in scripture), which is to convince ourselves that God is dissatisfied with us and will not work through us or answer our prayers until we reach that state of 'spiritual perfection'.

Last year our son, who is seven years old, had to undergo extensive orthopaedic surgery. Just when he needed his mother's prayers, I could not pray. I was afraid that if I did not pray well enough, then the operation would fail. I could not handle the responsibility and had to ask others to pray for him. I had forgotten the biblical account of the desperate man who brought his son to Jesus for healing. When Jesus said to him that everything is possible to those who believe, he cried, 'I do believe; help me overcome my unbelief!' (Mark 9:24, NIV) The boy was healed even though his father was struggling with spiritual problems.

Surely, then, God does not abandon us even when we know there are things in our lives which need to change. Some scholars agree, believing that our idea of perfection today differs from that in the Bible. We tend to see it as a state of sinlessness but one scholar believes the Bible interprets it as someone in a right relationship with God in worship and service (J.I. Packer, *New Bible Dictionary*). He reasons that perfection is something that can only be achieved in union with Christ (Colossians 1:28) and even then, only at his second coming or when we are with him in glory (Philippians 3:10–14). While it is right to try to grow in our Christian faith, it is 'dark counsel' to believe we can reach a state of spiritual perfection here on earth. What a relief!

Potential

We are fortunate to live in a beautiful part of the country, and in the spring we often go on a walk in the bluebell woods. If you look at the flowers individually, some of them have all their bells open along the stems. Their tops lean gently to one side, they give a sweet perfume and are perfect. The majority, however, are not like this. Some have no bells open, some only a few—they have not yet reached their full potential. We may think that this will spoil the overall impression, but not at all. If you take a few steps back and survey the whole scene, the sight is beautiful. The imperfections of the individual flowers are lost in the perfection of the entire spectacle. Even the flowers with only one or two bells open contribute to the picture.

Perhaps we can learn something from this. When we feel frustrated by our own shortcomings and those of our church we need to take a metaphorical step backwards to remember that God does not exclude us from his love or his divine plan until we 'get our act together'. Rather he takes us as we are and with his miraculous resurrection power makes something beautiful from all our shortcomings.

Ruth Leak belongs to the Hereford Corps of the Salvation Army, where she and her family are involved in the band. She has contributed to a book of school assembly material and written for *Woman Alive*.

Beauty from Ashes

Jennifer Rees Larcombe

When my life seemed burnt to ashes, the last thing I could cope with was reading lengthy Bible passages, yet the Bible contains many verses which encourage and comfort people who are grappling with grief and loss. I began collecting these verses and sticking them all over my kitchen walls! My favourite verse reminded me that God could transform the ashes of my life into something new and beautiful. This book grew out of my collection of 'kitchen verses', combined with some of the practical tips and helpful ideas for those adjusting to loss of various kinds, given to me at the time by others who know how it feels from personal experience.

Beauty from Ashes, new from Jennifer Rees Larcombe and published by BRF, is a book for keeping by the bedside, for dipping into just for a few moments every day, offering help along the way for the hardest of times. You can find further details on page 154, and an order form on page 157.

Introduction

The day I began writing this book, my kitchen looked a mess! The walls and cupboard fronts were covered in scraps of paper, dusty and curling at the edges. Over the last four years, I've been sticking them there at the rate of several a week. I started the habit on the day that I still think of as the worst day of my life. I had often said a prayer that sounded something like this: 'Lord, I could cope with anything—except *that*. If that worst fear of mine were ever to happen, I would be finished, finally and completely.'

But it happened. My worst fear became an ugly, messy reality. During the last four years, I have experienced all the bizarre stages of the grieving process—the shock, rage, depression, the 'whys', 'what if's and 'if only's, the panic attacks, the loneliness and that awful longing for death and oblivion. But actually I'm not 'finished, finally and completely'! In fact I've discovered that God never allows us to go through our worst dread without giving us the strength to cope with it. More than that, he can actually use the experience to bless us profoundly. (Of course, I would have hit anyone who told me that when the mess was at its worst!)

As a trained counsellor, I understood all those ghastly stages of grief. Yet knowing what was happening to me did not help me much at all. It was those scraps of paper on my kitchen wall that kept me plodding along through my grief journey.

God has hidden, throughout the entire Bible, little phrases, promises and statements that I call the treasures of darkness (Isaiah 45:3). Reeling with shock and positively ill with grief, there was no way I could read long passages from the Bible. But, when I woke early in the morning, feeling utterly lost and far too afraid to face the day, I would get up, make a mug of tea and sit in my rocking-chair. I couldn't concentrate enough to pray, I couldn't feel God's presence, but I used to sit gripping my Bible as if it were God's hand. Whenever I opened it and took a short peep inside, he seemed to cause one of these 'treasures of darkness' to catch my eye. It was uncanny the way they always seemed to speak directly to me about the way I felt that particular day. Because my brain was unable to hold on to anything for more than two minutes, I used to scribble them down on scraps of paper—and so they arrived on my kitchen wall. As I waited for the kettle to boil, or the microwave to ping, I would read that day's acquisition over and over again, often feeling like a drowning man clinging to a life-belt.

At first, of course, I did not realize that it is not enough to decorate the place with comforting little verses and nice promises from God; you actually have to believe them! For me, the 'crunch' came after several weeks of verse collecting. It was late at night and I was huddled under my duvet, on the sofa, quite overwhelmed by fear and an awful sense of desolation. I was too afraid to go to bed because there was a mouse in my wardrobe! That morning a friend had written to me saying, 'Take a look at Isaiah 54.' At that moment, reading the Bible was about the last thing I wanted to do, but anything was better than lying there, stiff with anxiety. So I found the place, and suddenly, this verse jumped right off the page!

Your maker is your husband.' (Isaiah 54:5)

In other words, God was telling me that he was taking on the responsibility of caring for me, providing, protecting, cherishing and meeting all my needs, both practical and emotional. I remember lying there, curled up tight as a ball, and realizing I had a choice. I could either take God at his word and abandon myself to his love completely, or I could turn my back on him in disbelief.

'Take it or leave it!' I thought as I slowly crept out from under the duvet. I found a pen and paper and wrote the verse out, adding another from further down the page:

'Though the mountains be shaken and the hills be removed, yet my unfailing love for you will not be shaken nor my covenant of peace be removed', says the Lord, who has compassion on you. (Isaiah 54:10, NIV)

It felt as if I was making a very special pact with God as I stuck the paper in the place of honour over the kitchen sink. When I look up at it, I realize that the decision to believe it was the turning point in my recovery.

When I decided to write a book for people who are recovering from all kinds of loss, I realized that the best I could do was to share my 'scraps of paper' with them, hoping they would find them as much help as I had done. As I began pulling these scraps off the walls and cupboards, I remembered I also had a bundle of cards and letters that friends had sent me over the four years. I had stored them carefully away in the bottom drawer of my desk and soon I was sitting on the floor, with piles of paper laid out all around me. I felt as if I had discovered a gold mine!

Many described their own experiences, or shared verses, quotations or coping strategies that had helped them. After making this discovery, I remembered all the other 'treasures of darkness' I had collected when my life had exploded into painful fragments on a previous occasion. Back in the 1980s, I had been seriously ill with a brain virus that had left me in constant pain and, for eight long years, dependent on a wheelchair. God had undoubtedly mended my life that time too, and soon another 'gold mine' of cards, verses and slips of paper was unearthed from a tea chest in the attic.

If you feel your life has been shattered by some destructive experience—or you have lost someone you love, your financial security, mobility, health, reputation, a satisfying role or your plans and dreams for the future—all I can say is, 'God is in the business of mending people.' He has done that for me twice now, and I've seen him do it for too many other people to doubt his ability. The only thing he needs is for us to give him all the pieces of our broken hearts and lives, and to trust him to put us back together again in his own way and at his own pace.

Now that I am beginning to emerge into a completely new life, I know for certain that God really can create beauty from the ashes of our ruined lives when we ask him to do so.

Where are you, God?

Who is among you who reverently fears the Lord, who obeys the voice of his Servant, yet who walks in darkness and deep trouble and has no shining splendour in his heart? Let him rely on, trust in, and be confident in the name of the Lord, and let him lean upon and be supported by his God.

Isaiah 50:10 (Amp)

This was the very first verse to go up on my kitchen wall and I slapped it up there late in the evening of that dreaded day when I lost the person I love most in this world. I had rung a friend with the news long after her bedtime, but she had jumped straight into her car to bring me the verse written out on a card.

Some people say that they feel wonderfully 'carried' by God during those first few days or even weeks of loss, wafted along high above the earth and its horrible realities, on a golden cloud. I didn't. I felt nothing at all. There was no 'shining splendour' in my heart—or anywhere else for that matter. I spent my time mindlessly clearing out the garage, tidying the attic and sorting endless cupboards, late into the night. I did not cry, rage or worry about the future—until later!

When we are injured physically and pain becomes unbearable, the body has a way of sliding into unconsciousness. Perhaps that numb feeling I experienced (and even the 'cloud nine' euphoria reported by others) is rather similar. Our mind needs space to work through the implications of what has happened, so it switches off the emotions and renders us incapable of feeling anything.

This strange, detached state carries us over the worst part of our trauma, but while it saves us from feeling the bad emotions, it also cuts out the good ones. That is why it is often so hard to feel close to God after our lives have exploded. Prayer feels unsatisfying, reading the Bible is boring, and when we do pluck up enough courage to walk into church we might as well be singing nursery rhymes as hymns or praise songs to God.

When we realize that the 'shining splendour' in our hearts is missing, we panic. 'Just when I need God most, he's vanished', we mutter furiously. But here's another of my kitchen verses:

Never will I leave you; never will I forsake you. (Hebrews 13:5, NIV)

That is a promise. We will always have his presence with us, but nowhere does he promise that we will always *feel* it. It is the *fact* of his presence that matters.

On a cold, grey, foggy day in January, no one doubts that the sun is shining up there in the sky, beyond the wintry clouds. We can't see it or feel its warmth but, even though our teeth are chattering and we have to switch the lights on at midday, we are still sure the sun is there, simply because it always is!

A PRAYER

Lord, I feel desolate. Most of what I valued is gone. Loss surrounds me—loss in all directions—leaving me cut off, alone, unprotected. All I can hear are the echoes of familiar voices and laughter from the past. The memories of all the things I wanted to do, places I wanted to visit, people I wanted to meet, merely mock me now. Worst of all, I feel I've lost you too, God. Where are you?

God himself has said:

I will not in any way fail you nor give you up nor leave you without support. I will not, I will not, I will not in any degree leave you helpless nor forsake nor let you down (relax my hold on you)! Assuredly not!' (Hebrews 13:5, Amp)

Other Christina Press titles

Who'd Plant a Church? Diana Archer
£5.99 in UK
Planting an Anglican church from scratch, with a team of four—two adults and two children—is an unusual adventure even in these days. Diana Archer is a vicar's wife who gives a distinctive perspective on parish life.

Pathway Through Grief edited by Jean Watson
£6.99 in UK
Ten Christians, each bereaved, share their experience of loss. Frank and sensitive accounts offering comfort and reassurance to those recently bereaved. Jean Watson has lost her own husband and believes that those involved in counselling will also gain new insights from these honest personal chronicles.

God's Catalyst Rosemary Green
£8.99 in UK
Rosemary Green's international counselling ministry has prayer and listening to God at its heart. Changed lives and rekindled faith testify to God's healing power. Here she provides insight, inspiration and advice for both counsellors and concerned Christians who long to be channels of God's Spirit to help those in need.

God's Catalyst is a unique tool for the non-specialist counsellor; for the pastor who has no training; for the Christian who wants to come alongside hurting friends.

'To read this book will be helpful to any Christian interested in helping others.' *John White*

Angels Keep Watch Carol Hathorne
£5.99 in UK
A true adventure showing how God still directs our lives, not with wind, earthquake or fire, but by the still, small voice.

'Go to Africa.' The Lord had been saying it for over fory years. At last, Carol Hathorne had obeyed, going out to Kenya with her husband. On the eastern side of Nairobi, where tourists never go, they came face to face with dangers, hardships and poverty on a daily basis, but experienced the joy of learning that Christianity is still growing in God's world.

Not a Super-Saint Liz Hansford
£6.99 in UK

'You might have thought Adrian Plass… had cornered the market in amusing diary writing. Well, check out Liz Hansford's often hilarious account of life as a Baptist minister's wife in Belfast. Highly recommended.' *The New Christian Herald*

Liz Hansford describes the outlandish situations which arise in the Manse, where life is both fraught and tremendous fun. *Not a Super-Saint* is for the ordinary Christian who feels they must be the only one who hasn't quite got it all together. The message is, 'You are not alone.'

The Addiction of a Busy Life Edward England
£5.99 in UK

Twelve lessons from a devastating heart attack. Edward, a giant of Christian publishing in the UK, and founder of Christina Press, shares what the Lord taught him when his life nearly came to an abrupt end. Although not strictly a Christina title (Edward lacks the gender qualifications), we believe you may want to buy this for the busy men in your lives.

'A wonderful story of success and frailty, of love and suffering, of despair and hope. If you are too busy to read this book, you are too busy.' *Dr Michael Green*

Life Path Luci Shaw
£5.99 in UK

Personal and spiritual growth through journal writing. Life has a way of slipping out of the back door while we're not looking. Keeping a journal can enrich life as we live it, and bring it all back later. Luci Shaw shows how a journal can also help us grow in our walk with God.

Precious to God Sarah Bowen
£5.99 in UK

Two young people, delighted to be starting a family, have their expectations shattered by the arrival of a handicapped child. And yet this is only the first of many difficulties to be faced. What was initially a tragedy is, through faith, transformed into a story of inspiration, hope and spiritual enrichment.

All the above titles are available from Christian bookshops everywhere, or in case of difficulty, direct from Christina Press using the order form on page 156.

Other Bible Reading Fellowship titles

Beauty from Ashes Jennifer Rees Larcombe
Readings for times of loss
£5.99 in UK
'When my life seemed burnt to ashes, the last thing I could cope
with was reading lengthy Bible passages, yet the Bible contains
many verses which encourage and comfort people who are grappling with grief and loss. I began collecting these verses and
sticking them all over my kitchen walls! My favourite verse
reminded me that God could transform the ashes of my life into
something new and beautiful.'

This is a book for keeping by the bedside, for dipping into just
for a few moments every day, offering help along the way for the
hardest of times.

*'Through many struggles of her own, Jen has developed an amaz-
ing capacity to get to the heart of the matter. I am sure this book will
be invaluable to many hurting people' (Fiona Castle)*

In the Palm of God's Hand Wendy Bray
A diary of living against the odds
£5.99 in UK
'Sharing a diary like this is about more than baring your soul. It's
like taking your clothes off in public in mid-January and asking
passers-by to throw snowballs at you. Not something you would
do unless you hoped an awful lot of good would come of it. But
here I am, doing it (sharing the diary, that is—I'm too much of a
coward to attempt the illustration!) So I must believe in the
good. Whatever good might result is God's to reveal. I would
hope that it will involve glory to him and comfort and encouragement to others, as well as providing the occasional laugh.'

This prayer diary testifies how personal faith can transform
the hardest of times, and how God's love and mercy still break
through, no matter how tough the situation.

*'This is a book about trust… the kind that trusts God—anyway—
sometimes because there is just nowhere else to go.' (Rob Parsons)*

Taking Hold of Life Margaret Killingray
Deciding on right and wrong in today's world
£5.99 in UK
'Should I give up my career to care for my mother?'

'Should I forgive my husband for a one night stand?'

'Should we build a new conservatory when people elsewhere are starving?'

How do we go about making decisions, especially in a so-called 'grey area' where no choice seems ideal? How can the Bible really help us in choosing between right and wrong? *Taking Hold of Life* explores the influences that shape our thinking and the difficulty of making moral decisions in the real world, especially for Christians who have to learn to negotiate the tensions between their own feelings and weaknesses, the pressures of today's culture and God's law of love.

'*Full of practical wisdom for making the most of life.*' (Rob Warner)

Affirming Love Christine Leonard
Reflections into the heart of God
£5.99 in UK
Do you really believe that God loves you as well as knowing in your mind that he does?

This book aims to reach the hearts of all of us who have found it hard to feel God's love. The word of God interpreted through images, stories, poetry and meditations feeds and stimulates the mind, senses, spirit and emotions, soaking us in the wonder of his love, both in the normal course of life and in dark times.

Because God's love is so huge, we can't experience it all at once. Breaking it down into different aspects splits the dazzle of its white light into a rainbow of colours which can more readily be examined and enjoyed. Each new chapter is like the turning of a prism. Each colour may help us to see part of his love in a fresh way.

All the above titles are available from Christian bookshops everywhere or, in case of difficulty, direct from BRF using the order form on page 157.

Christina Press Publications Order Form

All of these publications are available from Christian bookshops everywhere or, in case of difficulty, direct from the publisher. Please make your selection below, complete the payment details and send your order with payment as appropriate to:

Christina Press Ltd
17 Church Road
Tunbridge Wells
Kent
TN1 1LG

		Qty	Price	Total
8700	God's Catalyst	____	£8.99	____
8702	Precious to God	____	£5.99	____
8703	Angels Keep Watch	____	£5.99	____
8704	Life Path	____	£5.99	____
8705	Pathway Through Grief	____	£6.99	____
8706	Who'd Plant a Church?	____	£5.99	____
8708	Not a Super-Saint	____	£6.99	____
8705	The Addiction of a Busy Life	____	£5.99	____

POSTAGE AND PACKING CHARGES				
	UK	Europe	Surface	Air Mail
£7.00 & under	£1.25	£2.25	£2.25	£3.50
£7.10–£29.99	£2.25	£5.50	£7.50	£11.00
£30.00 & over	free	prices on request		

Total cost of books   £ _____
Postage and Packing   £ _____
TOTAL   £ _____

All prices are correct at time of going to press, are subject to the prevailing rate of VAT and may be subject to change without prior warning.

Name _____

Address _____

_____ Postcode _____

Total enclosed £ _____ (cheques should be made payable to 'Christina Press Ltd')

☐ Please send me further information about Christina Press publications

BRF Publications Order Form

All of these publications are available from Christian bookshops everywhere or, in case of difficulty, direct from the publisher. Please make your selection below, complete the payment details and send your order with payment as appropriate to:

BRF, Peter's Way, Sandy Lane West, Oxford OX4 6HG

		Qty	Price	Total
124 X	Beauty from Ashes	_____	£5.99	_____
196 7	In the Palm of God's Hand	_____	£5.99	_____
194 0	Taking Hold of Life	_____	£5.99	_____
052 9	Affirming Love	_____	£5.99	_____

POSTAGE AND PACKING CHARGES	UK	Europe	Surface	Air Mail
£7.00 & under	£1.25	£2.25	£2.25	£3.50
£7.10–£29.99	£2.25	£5.50	£7.50	£11.00
£30.00 & over	free	prices on request		

Total cost of books £ _____
Postage and Packing £ _____
TOTAL £ _____

All prices are correct at time of going to press, are subject to the prevailing rate of VAT and may be subject to change without prior warning.

Name _____

Address _____

_____

_____ Postcode _____

Total enclosed £ _____ (cheques should be made payable to 'BRF')

Payment by: cheque ❏ postal order ❏ Visa ❏ Mastercard ❏ Switch ❏

Card no. ☐☐☐☐ ☐☐☐☐ ☐☐☐☐ ☐☐☐☐ ☐☐☐☐

Card expiry date ☐☐☐☐   Issue number (Switch) ☐☐☐☐

Signature _____
(essential if paying by credit/Switch card)

❏ Please send me further information about BRF publications

Visit the BRF website at www.brf.org.uk

Subscription information

Each issue of *Day by Day with God* is available from Christian bookshops everywhere. Copies may also be available through your church Book Agent or from the person who distributes Bible reading notes in your church.

Alternatively you may obtain *Day by Day with God* on subscription direct from the Publishers. There are two kinds of subscription:

Individual Subscriptions are for four copies or less, and include postage and packing. To order an annual Individual Subscription please complete the details on page 160 and send the coupon with payment to BRF in Oxford. You can also use the form to order a Gift Subscription for a friend.

Church Subscriptions are for five copies or more, sent to one address, and are supplied post free. Church Subscriptions run from 1 May to 30 April each year and are invoiced annually. To order a Church Subscription please complete the details opposite and send the coupon to BRF in Oxford. You will receive an invoice with the first issue of notes.

All subscription enquiries should be directed to:

BRF
Peter's Way
Sandy Lane West
Oxford
OX4 6HG

Tel: 01865 748227
Fax: 01865 773150
E-mail: subscriptions@brf.org.uk.

Church Subscriptions

The Church Subscription rate for Day by Day with God will be £9.90 per person until April 2002.

☐ I would like to take out a church subscription for _____ (Qty) copies.

☐ Please start my order with the January/May/September 2002* issue. I would like to pay annually/receive an invoice with each edition of the notes*. (*Please delete as appropriate)

Please do not send any money with your order. Send your order to BRF and we will send you an invoice. The Church Subscription year is from May to April. If you start subscribing in the middle of a subscription year we will invoice you for the remaining number of issues left in that year.

Name and address of the person organising the Church Subscription:

Name _____

Address _____

_____

_____

Postcode _____ Telephone_____

Church _____ Name of Minister_____

Name and address of the person paying the invoice if the invoice needs to be sent directly to them:

Name _____

Address _____

_____

_____

Postcode _____ Telephone_____

Please send your coupon to:

BRF
Peter's Way
Sandy Lane West
Oxford
OX4 6HG

DBDWG0101   The Bible Reading Fellowship is a Registered Charity

Individual Subscriptions

☐ I would like to give a gift subscription (please complete both name and address sections below)

☐ I would like to take out a subscription myself (complete name and address details only once)

The completed coupon should be sent with appropriate payment to BRF. Alternatively, please write to us quoting your name, address, the subscription you would like for either yourself or a friend (with their name and address), the start date and credit card number, expiry date and signature if paying by credit card.

Gift subscription name _____

Gift subscription address _____

_____

_____ Postcode _____

Please send to the above for one year, beginning with the May 2002 issue:

	UK	Surface	Air Mail
Day by Day with God	☐ £11.55	☐ £12.90	☐ £15.15
2-year subscription	☐ £19.99	N/A	N/A

Please complete the payment details below and send your coupon, with appropriate payment, to **The Bible Reading Fellowship, Peter's Way, Sandy Lane West, Oxford OX4 6HG.**

Your name _____

Your address _____

_____

_____ Postcode _____

Total enclosed £ _____ (cheques should be made payable to 'BRF')

Payment by: cheque ☐ postal order ☐ Visa ☐ Mastercard ☐ Switch ☐

Card no. ☐☐☐☐ ☐☐☐☐ ☐☐☐☐ ☐☐☐☐

Card expiry date ☐☐☐☐   Issue number (Switch) ☐☐☐☐

Signature _____

(essential if paying by credit/Switch card)

NB: These notes are also available from Christian bookshops everywhere.

DBDWG0101   The Bible Reading Fellowship is a Registered Charity